MURDEROUS MINDS GERMANY

MURDEROUS MINDS GERMANY

International Serial Killers Encyclopedia

Book 1

ALAN R. WARREN

Copyright © 2024 Alan R. Warren
All rights reserved.

All rights reserved. No part of this book may be reproduced, scanned, or distributed in any printed or electronic form without permission of the author. The unauthorized reproduction of a copyrighted work is illegal. Criminal copyright infringement, including infringement without monetary gain, is investigated by the FBI and is punishable by fines and federal imprisonment. Please do not participate in or encourage the privacy of copyrighted materials in violation of the author's rights. Purchase only authorized editions.

House of Mystery Publishing

Seattle, Washington, USA

Vancouver, British Columbia, Canada

First Edition

ISBN (Paperback): 978-1-989980-34-7
ISBN (eBook): 978-1-989980-35-4

Cover design, formatting, layout, and editing by Evening Sky Publishing Services

Contents

Book Description	vii
Introduction	xi
1. Christman Genipperteinga	1
2. Peter Stumpp	5
Werewolf of Bedburg	
3. Anna Maria Zwanziger	9
Her Truest Friend	
4. Sophie Ursinus	15
5. Gesche Gottfried	19
6. Elisabeth Wiese	25
Angel Maker	
7. Friedrich Schumann	29
Terror of Falkenhagen Lake	
8. Peter Kürten	33
Vampire of Dusseldorf	
9. Karl Denke	55
Forgotten Cannibal	
10. Carl Grobmann	61
Berlin Bluebeard	
11. Fritz Haarmann	65
Butcher of Hanover	
12. Joachim Kroll	91
Man Eater	
13. Paul Ogorzow	95
S-Bahn Murderer	

14. Rudolf Pleil   101
    The Deathmaker

15. Jürgen Bartsch   109
    The Carnival Killer

16. Heinrich Pommerenke   113
    The Beast of the Black Forest

17. Olaf Däter   119
    The Granny Killer

18. Fritz Honka   123
    Hamburg's Redlight Killer

19. Erwin Hagedorn   129
    East German Bloodlust Murderer

20. Volker Eckert   133
    The Truckdriver Killer

21. Norbert Hans Poehlke   139
    The Hammer Killer

22. Wolfgang Schmidt   143
    The Pink Giant

23. Martin Ney   145
    The Masked Man

24. Marianne Nölle   153
    Angel of Mercy

25. Frank Gust   155
    The Rhine-Ruhr Ripper

26. Stephan Letter   159
    Angel of Death

Sources   163
About the Author   169
Also By Alan R. Warren   171

Book Description

Step into the abyss with this gripping series that unravels the chilling tales of serial killers worldwide. From the damp and foggy streets of Victorian London to the bustling metropolises of modern-day America, no corner of the globe is left unexplored. Each book in the series delves into a different region, offering a comprehensive look at the infamous serial killers who have left a trail of terror in their wake.

The *International Serial Killers Encyclopedia* series sheds light on the murderous minds of many killers, including their motivations, methods, and madness, through detailed research and explicit retelling of events. Some are notorious names that echo through history books, while others are lesser-known killers whose stories are no less harrowing. Each volume reveals a new layer of darkness.

Amidst the horror, there are tales of resilience and justice – the strength of survivors and the justice meted out by the tireless efforts of law enforcement. These stories are a compelling blend of true crime facts and psychological insight and a haunting journey through the twisted minds and deeds of serial killers from around the world. Prepare to be enthralled, horrified, and captivated as you delve into the shadows of the abyss.

Volume 1 of the *International Serial Killers Encyclopedia* series focuses on the most notorious serial killers from Germany. It contains many cases where the twisted minds and deeds of those who stalked the streets of Germany left a trail of fear and destruction in their wake.

From the infamous Fritz Haarmann, a.k.a. the "Butcher of Hanover," who preyed upon young boys with chilling brutality, to Peter Kürten, a.k.a. the "Vampire of Dusseldorf," whose thirst for blood knew no bounds. Each chapter reveals the brutal tales of individuals consumed by their darkest desires and a compelling blend of true crime and psychological intrigue.

Murderous Minds Germany offers a chilling glimpse into the darkest recesses of the human psyche, reminding us that evil can lurk just beneath the surface, even in the most civilized society.

Introduction

HISTORY AND CRIME

In the quiet towns and bustling cities of Germany, beneath the veneer of order and civility, lies a haunting truth: the country has been home to some of the most notorious serial killers in history. From the chilling accounts of Fritz Haarmann, the "Butcher of Hanover," to the enigmatic saga of Peter Kürten, the "Vampire of Düsseldorf," Germany's landscape has been stained with the blood of innocents by those who walked among us, concealed by their ordinary façades.

Murderous Minds Germany meticulously examines these dark chapters in the nation's history. Through thorough research, psychological insight, and narrative skill, we embark on a journey into the minds of these evil individuals, exploring the depths of their depravity and the ripple effects of their actions.

Germany's history is marked by its cultural achievements, political turmoil, and the sinister presence of those who sought to unleash chaos upon its streets. As we delve into the stories of these serial killers, we confront the uncomfortable truths about human nature and the fragility of society's veneer of civility.

Each chapter of this book is a window into a different era, a different city, and a different killer. We bear witness to the horrors of Fritz Haarmann's reign of terror in post-World War I Hanover, where he lured young boys to their deaths with promises of work and shelter, only to butcher them in his apartment. We shudder at the calculated brutality of Peter Kürten, whose crimes sent shockwaves through the city of Düsseldorf and beyond, earning him the title of the "King of the Sexual Perverts."

But *Murderous Minds Germany* is not just a recounting of grisly deeds; it is also a testament to the resilience of the human spirit and the tireless pursuit of justice. Through the dedication of law enforcement officials, the courage of survivors, and the strength of communities, these monsters were brought to heel, and their reigns of terror were brought to an end.

As we turn the pages of this book, we are confronted with the uncomfortable truth that evil knows no boundaries and can manifest anywhere, even in the heart of a seemingly civilized society. But in confronting these truths, we also reaffirm our commitment to vigilance, empathy, and the belief that, even in the darkest times, there is always hope.

ONE

Christman Genipperteinga

Christman Genipperteinga was a serial murderer in the last half of the 1500s who was believed to have killed as many as nine hundred and sixty-four people (964). He was said to have been actively committing these murders for over twelve years, from 1569 to 1581.

Most of his story was written in a book published in 1581.

The only thing written about his childhood was that he lived in the Cologne, Germany, area and that he must have been born before 1569. Christman moved to an area known as Fraberg, and his house was built on top of a hill that overlooked the main road that traveled through the town. It was said that this gave him a good view of those traveling through the city. From there, he would size up his prey and make his plan to rob and kill them.

Christman had also forced a woman traveling from the Rhine River to Trier to live with her brother and live with him as a wife. He would force himself sexually on her for over seven years. She would remain chained up at the house whenever he left to do something. During their years together, she would have six of his children, but Christman would kill them at birth. It was reported that he would hang his dead children's bodies.

Christman eventually allowed his wife to leave the house and meet other people. She would tell the local Mayor about what she had lived through. The Mayor rounded up thirty men from the town who went to Christman's house and arrested him.

While searching his house, they found over seventy thousand dollars in money and other items.

During the trial, Christman's diary was shown to the court. It had a detailed listing of the nine hundred and sixty-four murders he had committed and what items he was able to steal from them. He admitted to each of the murders.

Christman was found guilty and sentenced to death by the wheel. He would be tortured while on the wheel by having pieces of his flesh torn from him and different bones broken from striking blows to his body.

TWO

Peter Stumpp

WEREWOLF OF BEDBURG

Peter Stumpp, sometimes known as Peter Stumpf, was believed to have been born in Bedberg, Germany, on October 31, 1530. However, no concrete evidence of his birth has been found. He used several aliases, such as Abal Griswold, Abil Griswold, and Ubel Griswold. There were rumors that Stumpp was never his real name and that people only called him this because his left hand had been removed, leaving only a stump.

As with many people living back then, not much of their young life was recorded anywhere, so little is known about it. His family was wealthier than the average family in that area as they were successful farmers.

Later in life, he had two children, a girl named Sybil and a boy whose name was unknown. How he came to have two children or if he had a wife, and if so, what happened to her has never been known.

During these times, Germany was the witch execution capital of Europe, where they had killed somewhere around thirty thousand people who were accused of being witches. The communities were scared of witchcraft and were always looking for anyone who exhibited any strange behavior. Peter Stumpp became one of those whose neighbors reported to the police as they found he acted strangely.

There had been a series of cow mutilations taking place throughout the Cologne area between 1564 and 1589. Rumors began that it was a wolf-like creature that had been attacking the farm animals of the region. Soon, these stories evolved into a werewolf. During one of these attacks on the cows, the ranchmen caught a wolf, and it was said they cut off its left paw. Soon, it became a werewolf with no left hand. Since Peter Stumpp had no left hand, he was believed to be the werewolf.

Stumpp was arrested and, under threat of

being stretched on the rack, he admitted to practicing witchcraft, lycanthropy, and necromancy since he was twelve years old.

During his confession, Stumpp also claimed to have met the devil once, who gave him a magical belt that would allow him to transform into a wolf anytime he wanted. Stumpp also said that during his time of being a werewolf, he had murdered at least sixteen people and raped several women, including his daughter. When the court asked to see his powerful belt, he said that he had returned it to the devil so that none of them could have it.

During his trial, Stumpp admitted to killing his only son while being a werewolf as well. He described in great detail how he ate the brains from his head during the attack.

Stumpp was found guilty of his crimes, and he was to be executed according to the laws of the time. He was tied to a giant wheel, and while it turned, his bones were broken in several places from blows with the backside of an axe. At the same time, others were ripping pieces of his flesh off of his body by using red-hot grips that looked like large tweezers. They would finally kill Stumpp by beheading him with an axe. To deter others from practicing any witchcraft, they placed

Stumpp's head on a spear and mounted it publicly so everyone could see it.

Along with Stumpp, they also executed his daughter and his girlfriend at the time for knowing about his crimes and not telling the police. They would be flayed and then strangled.

THREE

Anna Maria Zwanziger

HER TRUEST FRIEND

Anna Margaretha Zwanziger was born Anna Schonleben in Nuremberg, Rome, on August 7, 1760. Not much is known about her childhood except that she was orphaned by the age of five and lived with different relatives for several years until she reached the age of ten.

An unknown rich person became Anna's

guardian, paying for a good education. That same sponsor also arranged for Anna to marry a thirty-year-old lawyer named Zwanziger just after her fifteenth birthday.

They had two children, and her husband had become so severely addicted to alcohol that it resulted in his inability to work anymore. Her husband's inability to work led Anna to have to make money in any way that she could, including prostitution. Anna never worked in the streets and was only available to wealthy clients, usually doctors, lawyers, or judges.

Her husband died from complications of his alcoholism in 1796, leaving her alone with their two children. Anna continued to live as a prostitute until she became pregnant and had a baby girl. She later gave the baby up for adoption, but the baby girl died at the orphanage before being adopted out to new parents. After this, she ended her days as a prostitute.

Anna turned to housekeeping for some of the wealthy clients she had met while being a prostitute. She hated doing house cleaning and thought of herself above it. Yet she continued this kind of work for the next twenty years.

After she turned fifty years old, Anna became bitter from working for her more affluent bosses.

She thought she was better than them and deserved to be the house owner, not just the maid. At first, Anna planned to kill the wife of one of the judges who employed her and then try to get the judge to fall in love with her and marry her. But she was not attracting any of the men she had wanted because of the way she kept herself and her advancing age.

On March 5, 1808, Anna got a job with Judge Wolfgang Glaser at his house in Bavaria. Glaser had recently been separated from his wife, so she jumped at the opportunity and took the job. Anna thought that this was finally her chance to act on her plans. Unfortunately, Glaser's wife returned to the home before she had enough time to complete her plan. So Anna poisoned her wife, making her very ill, and she died about a month later.

Anna was eventually fired from the Glaser household and found work with a different judge named Grohmann in Sanspaareil. This judge was only thirty-eight years old but not in good health. She nursed him back to health only to be rejected by him. Grohmann suddenly became unwell again and died on May 8, 1809.

Anna then got another job for Judge Gebhard and his wife, who was pregnant at the time of her hiring. Gebhard's wife had her baby on May 13,

1809, and the mother and child were healthy. However, his wife became sick about three days later and died within a week of becoming ill.

Anna remained the judge's housekeeper after his wife's death. But rumors began circulating that Anna was somehow bad luck as everybody she worked for seemed to get sick and die. Some even said that death followed Anna everywhere she went.

Near the end of Summer, on August 25, 1809, when Judge Gebhard was having two other judges over for a formal dinner, his guests became ill. Soon after, several household staff also became sick with the same type of illness. Just one week later, when Gebhard was having another dinner party, his guests became ill throughout the night.

Later that night, after the party was over, Gebhard, suspicious of Anna, decided to fire her. The following day, before Anna left the house, she was seen filling the salt box in the kitchen. The other staff noticed this because it was never Anna's job. That same day, everyone in the household became sick. Gebhard sent for the police to investigate.

Police took some of the salt to examine it and found it was full of arsenic. The police arrested Anna. When her items were searched, they found packets of arsenic. They exhumed her previous employer, Glaser's wife, and found that her body had arsenic in it.

Anna was charged. Eventually, it was discovered that she had poisoned people who she worked for, and three had died. Anna was poisoning her employers with mild doses of arsenic, enough to make them sick but not die. She would spend all of her time caring for and nursing her victims back to health, hoping it would put her in a good light with her employers and their friends.

Anna Zwanziger was convicted of four murders in total and sentenced to death. She was executed by sword.

FOUR

Sophie Ursinus

Sophie Charlotte Elisabeth Ursinus, nee Weingarten, was born in Glatz, Lower Silesia, Prussia, now called Klodzko, Poland, on May 5, 1760. Her father was an Austrian Legation secretary who lost his position when Germany annexed their city. When Sophie was only nineteen, she married Theodor Ursinus, a much older Supreme Court Counselor. One day after his birthday, on September 11, 1800, Theodor died suddenly of what doctors believed was tuberculosis. Much of his family was angry with Sophie as she didn't call for a doctor for two days after he became sick.

Before Theodor died, when he was stationed in Berlin, Sophie began an affair with a much younger man, a Dutch officer named Rogay. Sophie later claimed that her much older husband had given her permission to have the affair. But Rogay, too, died of what doctors thought was tuberculosis.

One year later, Sophie's aunt died after being sick with bad stomach cramps for a few days. She left Sophie a large inheritance. Two years after that, Sophie's servant, Benjamin Klein, became very ill with stomach pain. She gave him an emetic to relieve his stomach pain and then some soup. But he got even worse, and Benjamin became suspicious. Afterward, while resting in his room, Sophie brought him some fruit. Instead of eating them, he arranged to have them examined by a chemist. It was discovered that the plums were poisoned with arsenic.

After reporting the poisoned fruit to the police,

Sophie was arrested. Detectives began to think she possibly had poisoned her husband as well, so they exhumed his body to perform an autopsy. The medical examiners could not conclusively say that her husband had been poisoned with arsenic. Still, there was suspicion since the condition of his organs showed that he likely had been poisoned.

Police also exhumed Sophie's aunt's body as well to do an autopsy. This time, it was conclusive that she had been poisoned with arsenic.

Sophie was tried and convicted of the murder of her aunt as well as the attempted murder of her servant. She was sentenced to life imprisonment.

In 1833, Sophie was given a pardon after serving thirty years. She was accepted back into Glatz's high society as if she had never been in jail. She died three years later, in 1836.

FIVE

Gesche Gottfried

Gesina "Gesche" Margarethe Timm and her twin brother, Johann Timm Jr., were born in Bremen, Germany, on March 6, 1785. Their parents worked in the garment business: their mother, Gesche Margarethe, was a seamstress, and their father, Timm Sr, was a tailor. They lived a very modest life with little money.

When Gesche turned twenty-one, she married Johan Mittenberg, a saddler, and they had three children together. When Johan's father died and left him an inheritance, it allowed him to quit working. He started going out every night and drinking until late at night before returning home. By 1813, he had spent all of the money they inherited.

Within two months, Johan suddenly died after having severe stomach pain. A few months later, Gesche met and started dating a wealthy wine merchant, Michael Christoph Gottfried. The two were eventually married, but in the end, he died as well. Her family members also died, one after the other, from the same ailments: Gesche's mother, her three children, and her father.

Around this time, Germany was experiencing a large cholera outbreak, and Gesche became a nurse and supporter of several patients in Breman, earning the nickname "Angel of Bremen." It was during the epidemic that Gesche's family died, and when her family members died, she received a lot of sympathy from many of the people in her neighborhood. Many other deaths occurred that weren't scrutinized by a doctor or any medical professionals. Most were presumed to have happened because of the cholera outbreak.

Early in 1826, Gesche decided to sell her home to Johan and Wilhelmina Rumpff, but she agreed to remain their housekeeper. By the Summer of that same year, Wilhelmina became ill and died. A few months later, Johan also became sick.

Johan began to suspect his new maid, Gesche. He started to examine everything he was going to eat or drink. A few days later, he noticed what looked like specks of white powder on his food. Instead of eating it, he scraped some of the white stuff off his food and took it to a chemist to see if he should be worried about it.

The doctor who analyzed the white stuff that Johan had found on his food reported that it was arsenic, and they reported the finding to the police.

Gesche had heard about the finding of arsenic before the police were notified, and she fled to Hanover. Once there, it wasn't long before she became a maid for another household where, eventually, their family members would begin to die as well.

The Hanover police arrested Gesche on March 6, 1828, her forty-third birthday, after they discovered that the family she was cooking for had died of poisoning. Once arrested and confronted with the evidence of poisonings, she admitted to killing fifteen people and trying to kill many others, including both her parents, both of her husbands, a fiancé, and all three of her children.

Gesche Gottfried was tried and convicted of the murders and sentenced to death by decapitation. She was executed by guillotine on April 21, 1831, in Bremen, which was the last execution carried out in that city.

Gesche Gottfried mainly used homemade rat poison, which consisted of tiny flakes of arsenic mixed into the fat from animal meat. Her modus operandi was to start her victims off with small doses, which just made them feel ill, sort of like they had the flu. Then, she agreed to care for them through their "sickness." She relished getting praise and sympathy from others. Eventually, the victim would die, and she would move on to another.

Many believe that she had "Munchausen Syndrome by Proxy," which is a pervasive disorder among female serial killers. They enjoy the praise and care from others over their grief and hardship, so much so that they start doing it regularly to get the ecstasy-like feeling it gives them.

Gesche Gottfried list of murders:

1. Johann Mittenberg, her first husband, on October 1, 1813.
2. Gesche Margarethe Timm, her mother, on May 2, 1815.
3. Johanna Gottfried, her daughter, on May 10, 1815.
4. Adelheid Gottfried, her daughter, on May 18, 1815.
5. Johann Timm, her father, on June 28, 1815.
6. Heinrich Gottfried, her son, on September 22, 1815.
7. Johann Timm, her brother, on June 1, 1816.
8. Michael Christoph Gottfried, her second husband, on July 5, 1817.
9. Paul Thomas Zimmermann, her fiancé, on June 1, 1823.
10. Anna Lucia Meyerholz, friend, on March 21, 1825.
11. Johann Mosees, her neighbor, on December 5, 1826.

12. Wilhelmine Rumpff, her landlady and boss, on December 22, 1826.
13. Elise Schmidt, her friend's daughter, on May 13, 1827.
14. Beta Schmidt, friend, on May 15, 1827.
15. Fredrich Kleine, her friend and creditor, on July 24, 1827.

SIX

Elisabeth Wiese

ANGEL MAKER

lisabeth Wiese was a German baby farmer and serial killer convicted and executed for the murder of five children. She was born in Bilshausen, Germany, on July 1, 1853, but little is known about her early family life. She married Heinrich Wiese, had a daughter named Paula, and worked as a midwife who helped other poor women have babies. She had been a midwife from the time she was a teenager.

After that, she was caught giving abortions to women. A crime at the time, her conviction for this crime made it impossible for her to continue being a midwife. The family struggled financially, and her husband fought with her about her getting a different job to help pay for things around the house.

Wiese was angry with her husband for always yelling at her about spending money, so she decided that she would kill him. The first time she tried to kill him, she tried poisoning him, but it didn't work. Her second attempt didn't go much better. She waited until he was drunk and in a deep sleep when she grabbed a kitchen knife and tried slitting his throat. He awoke, and she was arrested for attempted murder and sent to prison for the crime.

When she was released from prison, Wiese established herself as a professional "foster mother." But, in truth, she was a baby farmer. She preyed on parents who were looking to adopt children because they were unable to have them naturally. Wiese would find poor mothers or mothers who had illegitimate children and needed to give them up. She would offer to find suitable adoptive parents for their children in good homes for a one-time fee.

Often, Wiese would find adoptive parents, charge them for their new child, and not pay the birth mother anything. But in some cases, when she couldn't find any adoptive parents to take the children or babies she had taken from the mothers, she poisoned them and burned their remains in her kitchen stove.

Eventually, a few reports came to the police that babies were missing who were supposed to be adopted. Detectives started to investigate Elisabeth, and she quit offering the service.

The end of her baby farming led to financial difficulties for her again, so she forced her daughter into prostitution. Her daughter became pregnant and gave birth to a child, and Wiese killed the baby and burned the remains in her stove like she did the others.

The police arrested Elisabeth and charged her with living off immoral earnings and the murder of five children. She was convicted and sentenced to death on October 10, 1904, and months later was executed by guillotine.

SEVEN

Friedrich Schumann
TERROR OF FALKENHAGEN LAKE

Friedrich Schumann was born in Spandau, Germany, a western borough of Berlin, on February 1, 1893. He lived with his father, a nasty alcoholic who had a criminal record that included everything from sexual assault to theft and robberies.

When Friedrich was only twelve years old, his father bought him his first rifle. He practiced his aim by shooting animals in the bush. It was during one of his target practices on animals when he hit and killed his female cousin. Even though he claimed it was an accident and that the gun went off accidentally, he was sent to a correctional facility for young boys. When he was released, he found a job working for a locksmith friend of his father's. Later, he was conscripted for the German army when World War I started in 1914. He became an excellent marksman and sniper for the military, winning an Iron Cross for his battle years.

When the war ended in 1918, he returned to regular life with his family but struggled, as many veterans did. He couldn't get a job or adjust to civilian life, so he turned to a life of crime.

Over the following three years, Friedrich committed seven murders, fifteen attempted murders, five arsons, eleven rapes, and an unknown amount of robberies of people and thefts from stores. He was arrested and charged with one of his murders, a fifty-two-year-old Wilhelm Nielbock, who was also from the same neighborhood as he was.

His trial began on July 5, 1920, lasted only one week, and ended in a conviction of murder. He was sentenced to the death penalty seven times over, one life sentence, and ten years of hard labor. Friedrich Schumann was executed by axe on the morning of August 27, 1921.

EIGHT

Peter Kürten
VAMPIRE OF DUSSELDORF

Peter Kürten was born in Mulheim am Rhein, Germany, on May 3rd, 1883, and was the oldest of thirteen children. His parents were both terrible alcoholics who couldn't hold a job and lived in poverty, with all fifteen members of the family living in a one-bedroom apartment.

Abuse was the norm for the whole family. Throughout his childhood, his drunken father would frequently beat his mother, as well as all of the kids. The abuse included times when his father would order his mother to take off all of her clothes. Once she was naked, he would have sex with her and make all of the kids watch.

After experiencing so much abuse at a young age, it wasn't long before Peter Kürten started abusing others as well. At only five years old, he tried to drown one of his friends, which caused his father to beat him into unconsciousness. Then, he became friends with a dog catcher who lived upstairs in the same apartment building as his family. He often went along with the animal control officer for something to do. The animal control officer would frequently beat, torture, and even kill many of the animals that he caught. Kürten began participating in the same behavior.

At an early age, Kürten often ran away from home for weeks, living on the streets and making friends with petty criminals and thieves. He soon started stealing things himself to get food and clothing. During one of those periods, Kürten later admitted to committing his first murder.

When he was only nine years old and playing on the river with two other boys, he pushed one of the boys, who couldn't swim, into the water. When the boy started to drown, the third boy that was with them jumped into the river to try and save him. Kürten followed him into the river after the third boy and held his head under the water until he drowned. Both boys died. The deaths would be ruled accidental at the time.

When Kürten turned thirteen, he started to date a girl the same age. The two of them would get naked and play with each other, but she wouldn't allow him to have intercourse with her. To relieve his sexual pressure, Kürten committed beastiality on animals such as sheep, pigs, and goats at the local farms. Years later, when Kürten was arrested, he admitted to stabbing some of the animals that he was having sex with, claiming the stabbing helped him achieve a more intense orgasm.

The following year when Kürten turned fourteen years old, he tried to rape his thirteen-year-old sister, the very sister that his father had molested several times when she was a younger girl. But he was stopped by their father.

Kürten's father got him a job with a moulder and made him quit school. He did very well learning the trade and worked for about two years until he decided to rob his boss' house, where he absconded with about 300 marks. Kürten took the money, left home, and moved to Koblenz. He met a prostitute and ended up living with her for about four weeks until he was arrested for the recent theft. He was convicted and sentenced to one month in jail.

Kürten was released from jail in November of 1899 and continued his life of crime. According to him, in a later confession, he picked up an eighteen-year-old girl, brought her home, and during sex with her, he strangled her to death with his bare hands. Police were unable to find any records of this woman's death.

In early 1900, Kürten's mother divorced his father and moved to Dusseldorf, where she started dating and remarried. Kürten ended up following her there. After only a few months, Kürten was arrested again, only this time it was for an attempted murder of a young woman. Later that year, Kürten was convicted and imprisoned for four years.

In July 1904, Kürten was released and drafted into the German Army. He was deployed to Metz, France, and assigned to the infantry division. Within a few months, Kürten deserted the army.

He returned to Dusseldorf and, before the end of that year, started at least twenty-four fires. Lighting buildings on fire sexually aroused Kürten, and he would sit back and watch as the firefighters came to the scene to fight the fires. Later in his confessions, Kürten claimed that he had a fantasy of watching some "tramps" burn alive while he watched.

It wasn't long before Kürten was caught and arrested by police, and along with being charged and convicted of twenty-four arsons, the military court also convicted him of desertion and sentenced him to serve eight more years in prison.

During those years in prison, he was regularly disciplined with beatings and placed in solitary confinement. He later told psychologists who studied him after his arrest that it was during this imprisonment that he developed fantasies of killing large groups of people at one time. For him, this fantasy was so pleasurable that he would often spontaneously ejaculate just thinking about it.

Murders

After serving his time for arsons and desertion and unbeknownst to the authorities what Kürten was truly capable of, in March 1913, he was released from prison. Shortly after that, on May 25th, he robbed a local tavern after they had closed up for the day. During the burglary, he went upstairs to check in the bedrooms for anything that he might like when he came across a nine-year-old girl, Christina Klein, sleeping in a bed. He strangled her to death and then pulled a knife out of his pocket and slashed the girl's throat. As her blood poured onto the floor, he masturbated.

The next day, Kürten went to another tavern across the street from the crime scene to listen to what people said about the crime. But Kürten told authorities later that he felt great disgust when he heard locals talk about and grieve the murder. He noticed it was the opposite of his thoughts and feelings during the attack. He also began going to the girl's grave to show respect. He claimed that he only had to touch the ground around the grave, and he spontaneously ejaculated from the feeling of elation.

While in Dusseldorf, Kürten acquired a skeleton key that could open several locks on house doors. He would then start looking for homes to burglarize late at night.

Two months after the murder of Christina Klein, he committed his next crime. He broke into a house and found a seventeen-year-old Gertrud Franken sleeping in her bed. Kürten strangled her with his bare hands and ejaculated again at the sight of blood coming from his victim's mouth. Gertrud did not die from the attack, but Kürten fled the scene. Just as with the Klein murder, he was not caught and arrested.

A few days later, Kürten was arrested and charged with another arson. He was convicted of all charges and, this time, sentenced to serve six years in a military prison. He repeated his insubordinate behavior in prison and again served most of his time in solitary confinement. In fact, Kürten's behavior was so bad that he received an additional two years on his sentence.

When Kürten was released from prison this time, he decided to live with one of his sisters in Altenburg. He got his first real job as a trade union official here. He also met a woman, Auguste Scharf, who owned a chocolate and sweets store. The two of them were married two years later. Like Kürten, his new wife also had her share of legal problems. Years earlier, not only was Scharf an active sex worker who had been arrested several times, but she had also been convicted of shooting her previous fiancé to death. During his marriage with Scharf, they would seldom have intercourse, likely because he liked to strangle the girls he was having sex with or needed to watch them bleed to have an orgasm.

Kürten could not make friends in Altenbrug, so after losing his union job in 1925, he moved back to Dusseldorf with his wife. After returning, he met two women who allowed him to strangle them while having sex. He wasn't killing them, just strangling them enough to be aroused. Once Scharf discovered that Kürten had been having these affairs, she became angry and spoke publicly about them. In response, both women claimed that he had seduced or raped them.

Kürten was again arrested, charged, and sentenced to an eight-month prison term. After agreeing to leave Dusseldorf, he was released after only six months. But after getting out, he successfully appealed the ruling that ordered him to leave Dusseldorf.

Kürten returned to Dusseldorf in early 1929, and by February, he attacked his first victim there. He spotted a forty-year-old woman, Apollonia Kuhn, out shopping one day, and he was instantly drawn to her. He followed her until she walked into a secluded, bushed area. He came from behind and threw his whole body weight on her, knocking her to the ground. He yelled at her not to scream, or he would kill her. He then dragged her into some bushes and stabbed her twenty-four times with a pair of scissors that he carried with him. He was so forceful with each stab that the scissors would get stuck into one of her bones. After he had an orgasm, he stopped stabbing, got up, and left the scene. Astonishingly, Kuhn didn't die from the brutal attack.

A mere five days later, on February 8th, 1929, Kürten struck again. This time, it was a nine-year-old girl named Rosa Ohliger. He spotted her walking through a small park located near a bridge. He grabbed her with one arm and swooped her up while his other hand covered her mouth. He dragged her into the park and choked her until she passed out. He then took out his scissors and began to stab her everywhere on her body, including her stomach, genitals, chest, and head. The stabbing had the same effect as his other victims, and he ejaculated while he was stabbing. But this time, Kürten gathered up as much of his semen as he could and put it into her vagina. He then dragged her body further into the park and placed it under some loose brush. Kürten went home, grabbed a kerosene lamp, and returned to the crime scene a few hours later. He lit Ohliger's body on fire. He stayed there, watching it burn until he had another orgasm before leaving. Her remains were found the following day.

Kürten struck again five days later, only this time he would attack a man: Rudolf Scheer, a forty-five-year-old mechanic who lived and worked in Dusseldorf's suburbs. Again, Kürten stabbed his victim twenty-one times in the head, back, and even the eyes. Kürten never said why he killed a man this time or if he had an orgasm while stabbing him. After Scheer was found murdered, Kürten went to the crime scene and talked with police, telling them that he had heard about the murder from a telephone call.

During their investigation of these three murders, the police decided that they were all connected, and they thought all had the same perpetrator. But the detectives couldn't find a motive for the murders as none of them had been robbed, and the victim's sex and age were varied.

Over the next five months, Kürten attempted to rape and strangle four other women, but none of them were killed.

On August 11th, Maria Hahn, a young woman Kürten had met three days earlier, agreed to date him. A few hours into their date, he asked her to walk him through a pretty field in a local park. Once the two of them found a quiet, remote spot, he attacked her sexually. During the attack, he pulled out a knife, and she began to scream and plead for her life. He strangled her until she passed out, then began to stab her until he had an orgasm. Kürten later admitted to having changed his weapon from his regular scissors to a knife to try and make the police believe that a different killer had murdered Hahn. After the brutal assault, he sat beside her body and waited for her to die, which took about one hour.

When Kürten arrived home to his wife, she noticed bloodstains on his jacket. He made up some story about finding a dead animal on the road, and he moved it to the bush and got some of its blood on him. Kürten started to worry that once police found the murdered girl, his wife might connect him because of the bloodstains. So he went back, moved her body to a cornfield, and buried her.

After a couple of weeks passed and she hadn't been discovered, Kürten got the idea that he should take Hahn's body and nail it to a tree in a sort of mock Jesus crucifixion in hopes of upsetting and revolting the community. Kürten went to the cornfield where he buried her remains, but after he dug up Hahn's body, he found it to be too heavy to lift to the tree to nail her there. So, he just returned her remains to the ground where he had initially buried her.

In November, Kürten wrote an anonymous letter to police telling them that he had murdered Hahn. He included a detailed map of how they could find where she had been buried, and they recovered Hahn's remains on November 15th.

After killing Hahn, Kürten decided to stab some more people randomly to cause confusion and create the idea that a different killer was on the loose. On the morning of August 21st, Kürten went to a different part of town in Dusseldorf. As he walked the neighborhood, he looked for people alone and in an area where no others were around. His first victim was an eighteen-year-old girl, his second was a thirty-year-old man, and his third and final victim was a thirty-seven-year-old woman. He just walked up to each one of them and, without saying a word, began stabbing them. All three of the victims were severely hurt, but none of them were sexually assaulted or killed.

Three days later, Kürten went to the Flehe fairgrounds and noticed two young girls leaving to go home. He approached them and offered the older girl twenty pfennig to go and buy him cigarettes. After she ran off to a store to get them, he grabbed the other girl by her neck and choked her until she passed out. He slit her throat with the same knife he had used before and tossed her body into some bush off the road. When the older girl returned to give Kürten the cigarettes, he grabbed her by her neck, partially strangled her, and then stabbed her in the chest. This time, though, he bit her on the neck and drank some of her blood. Neither girl was sexually assaulted.

The very next day, Gertrude Schulte, a twenty-seven-year-old maid, was walking home when Kürten approached her and asked her if she would have sex with him. When she said no and started to walk away from him, he turned, yelling at her, "Okay, then die," before pulling out his knife and stabbing her. Schulte was stabbed in her head, neck, back, shoulders, legs, and arms. He never sexually assaulted her. She survived the attack but couldn't give a perfect description of her attacker.

Kürten made two more knife attacks in September before deciding to change his murder weapon again. On the night of September 30th, he met Ida Reuter, a thirty-one-year-old maid, at a train station on her way home from work. He was very charming, and the two went to a coffee shop and talked for a while. After they left, he walked her along the riverfront. As soon as they were all alone, he pulled out a hammer and started to hit her on the head. She passed out, and he sexually assaulted her.

Two weeks later, Kürten struck again. He met twenty-two-year-old Elisabeth Dorner, another maid, outside a theatre where she had just watched a play alone. As he did with Reuter, Kürten charmed her into going to a café and walking along the riverfront. Once they were in a remote area with nobody else around, he pulled out his hammer and hit her on the head. She fell immediately. He sexually assaulted her as well. But this time, once he was finished, he hit her over and over on her head with the hammer. She was found the next day and remained in a coma until she died.

Kürten attacked two other women in the same way and with his hammer. Both were sexually assaulted, but neither woman died. On his second victim, his hammer broke during the attack, which may have saved her life. Kürten went back to his scissors.

Five-year-old Gertrude Albermann was walking alone two weeks later when Kürten saw her. He approached her and convinced her to walk to an abandoned community garden with him. Once they got there, he took out his scissors and began stabbing her in her head and face. Once the girl fell to the ground, he stabbed her thirty-four more times. He covered her body with some weeds from the garden and left.

Kürten made a great effort to make it look like several different murderers were committing these crimes by using various weapons and methods of attacking his victims. Despite his efforts, the police knew that there was only one killer. In 1929, the murders received so much press and were talked about in the city because most of the attacks were carried out with such savagery. The police used the press to ask for witnesses or leads, and in just one year, they received more than thirteen thousand leads and interviewed more than nine thousand people. In addition to these leads, Kürten could help himself by also sending letters.

The detectives weren't long figuring out that only one person was behind all these attacks in the city. Kürten's letters about murders using different weapons and different methods were in the same handwriting as the one he previously sent directing them where to find Christine Hahn's body. When the police document examiner and handwriting analyst reviewed the letters, they were determined to have been written by the same person.

During the next five months in 1930, Kürten assaulted ten more victims using a hammer. He assaulted and tried to strangle many of them as well, but none of the victims were killed.

On May 5th, 1930, Kürten spotted twenty-year-old Maria Budlick leaving a train alone. He approached her and, after learning that she was searching for a job and a place to live, offered to help her find a local hostel, telling her he knew the area well. Shortly after leaving the train station, Kürten invited her for food and a drink to an apartment he had rented, and she gladly accepted his offer.

At Kürten's apartment, they each had a drink, and he started to make sexual advances towards her, but she refused. After they had finished their drink, he told her he could take her to a hostel. They left his apartment, and Kürten led the way to what he said was a cheap but nice place for her to stay. About ten minutes into their walk, he led her to a wooded area, where he suddenly grabbed her throat and began to strangle her. They both fell to the ground, and he started to rip her clothes off her. Budlick got a chance to free her mouth and screamed at the top of her lungs, which startled Kürten. He let go of her, got up, and ran away.

Budlick didn't go to the police or report the attack. Instead, she just went about finding a place to rent and a new job. But once she was settled, she wrote to her friend back home, and in that letter, she told about the assault. When she posted the letter, she had incorrectly addressed it. The post office clerk opened it to determine where it should be sent. In that letter, he read about Budlick's assault and gave the letter to the police. Once the detectives read over the letter, they thought that it could be possible that Budlick was attacked by the killer they were looking for, so they found her and brought her in for an interview.

During the interview, Budlick could not remember the address of the man who attacked her, but she could take them to where he lived. Once there, police spoke to the landlord of the building and found out that a man named Kürten had been renting there. The detectives had the landlord bring them to Kürten's apartment, and they searched his room. While there, Kürten arrived home. He saw them and noticed they were with his victim, Budlick, so he fled.

Kürten immediately ran home to his wife. He was now scared that the police might think that he was the killer they referred to as the "Vampire of Dusseldorf" and began to panic. He sat his wife down and told her that he had attacked Budlick and that the police were looking for him. Kürten explained to her that he would probably get at least fifteen years in prison because he had been convicted of crimes like this before. He told his wife that he had to go away for a short time to figure out what to do.

Arrest

On May 23rd, Kürten returned home, but this time, he admitted to his wife that he was the "Vampire of Dusseldorf." He said she should turn him into the police and collect the reward. The next day, Kürten's wife went to the police station and told them that she had just found out that her husband was the murderer that they were looking for. Even though she was aware of his past crimes, when he had attacked some women, she never would have believed that he could commit all of those brutal murders. She had arranged for Kürten to turn himself in to the police, and they were to meet him at a church later that afternoon. He was there when they arrived, and they arrested him.

Kürten admitted that he was the murderer that they were looking for during his first interview with the police. He admitted to a total of sixty-eight crimes, including nine murders and thirty-one attempted murders. Kürten did not give any reasons or excuses for the murders he had committed but stated that the children he murdered did not suffer any.

The detectives and psychiatrists who spoke with Kürten learned that he needed at least the sight of blood to reach an orgasm, and after he reached his climax, he would often feel very sorry for the women. Kürten also told them that once he had killed a swan and drank the blood from its neck, which made him orgasm, and so he started doing the same with his human victims.

Trial

Peter Kürten's trial began on April 13, 1931, in Dusseldorf. Prosecutors charged him with nine murders and seven attempted murders. He pleaded not guilty on all charges due to reason of insanity. Throughout his trial, he was kept behind a cage that had been built specifically to keep him safe from being assaulted by anyone in the courtroom during his trial.

During the trial, the Judge asked Kürten why he confessed and whether it was just for the financial reward his wife would get for turning him in to the police. He responded by saying that he still loved his wife and she had never done anything wrong. She stood by him throughout all of his affairs with other women and previous prison sentences.

The Judge also asked Kürten if he had ever felt any regret for all the pain he had caused to the victims and their families. He responded by saying that he didn't feel bad at all and that he immensely enjoyed doing the murders. Kürten thought that he had no consciousness at all.

The prosecution had five very well-known psychiatrists and doctors to testify that Kürten was legally sane. In their opinions, Kürten had always been in complete control of his impulses and his actions. He killed the way he did because Kürten had an uncontrollable desire to achieve an orgasm, and the only way he could do this was while others were in pain. To achieve this, he would create an event.

The Defense contended that it was, in fact, the range of Kürten's perversions that led to his engagement in these brutal attacks and that proved his insanity.

Kürten's trial lasted ten days, and the jury only deliberated for two hours to reach the verdict. He was found guilty and sentenced to death for nine counts of murder and seven counts of attempted murder.

Kürten would not appeal the decision of his guilt but instead made a plea not to be executed. This appeal would later be denied, and he wrote letters of apology to each victim's relatives.

Execution

On July 2, 1931, at six in the morning, Peter Kürten was executed by the guillotine at the Klingelputz Prison located in Cologne, Germany. The night before, he was granted a final meal of Weiner schnitzel and white wine. After Kürten was executed, his brain was removed and given to scientists to try and figure out why he committed all of those crimes and why he behaved the way he did. Upon examination, there were no abnormalities found. His body was also examined, and nothing abnormal was found there either.

After World War II, his head was taken to the US and displayed at Ripley's Believe It or Not Museum in Wisconsin.

NINE

Karl Denke

FORGOTTEN CANNIBAL

Karl Denke was born in Oberkunzendorf, Prussia, now known as Ziebice, Poland, on February 11, 1860. Not much is known about Denke's childhood except that he did poorly in school and wouldn't listen to any of his teachers. At twelve, Denke quit school and ran away from home. In his youth, he worked as an apprentice gardener, and when he was twenty-five years old, he started his own gardening business.

When Denke's father passed away, he was left with some money. He used it to buy himself property. He began to farm on his property but hated it, so he quit and sold the land. With the money from selling his property, Denke decided to buy a rental property. This also didn't work out for him, so he sold the house. Denke then decided to open a meat shop, where he sold not only boneless meat but leather as well.

Denke joined the local church and became very well-liked in his community.

When Denke turned forty-three years old in 1903, for some unknown reason, he began murdering homeless people or beggars. The first known victim was twenty-five-year-old Emma Sander in 1909. Initially, someone else was convicted of her murder, but years later, when the truth came out, the other guy was released.

Throughout Denke's murder spree, he kept a list of his victims, including details on how he murdered them.

Denke's last known victim was Vincent Oliver on December 21, 1924. Denke told Oliver that he would write him a letter of reference and give him some money if he came to his house. The two men were sitting down at Denke's table, and he was writing a letter for Oliver when suddenly, Denke grabbed a pick axe and swung it at Oliver's head. Oliver quickly moved just in time and dodged the axe. The two fought, and Oliver was able to get a hold of the axe. He escaped from Denke's house, screaming something about a madman trying to kill him, and two police officers who were nearby came running. Denke was arrested.

Denke was placed in a cell at the jail until detectives could interrogate him. Before they could get a chance to, Denke hanged himself in his cell. At the time, several rumors circulated in the town that he had used his handkerchief or shoelaces, but the exact details were never released to the public.

After his death, while the police searched Denke's house, they found several pieces of human flesh that were in the process of being cured inside two tubs filled with brine. There was also a large wooden box filled with various human bones. Denke also had several cooking pots full of human fat. But the most shocking thing the police found in Denke's house was several items he had made from tanned human skin, such as shoelaces, shoes, braces, and belts.

The number of Denke's victims was never conclusively determined. All the police had to go on was the list of victims that Denke had made. There were thirty names on his list, but the police would later guess that Denke killed around forty-two people, given the number of body parts found in his apartment. Why he was keeping track of them on the list is still unknown.

The final list of what detectives found while searching Denke's apartment was released about six months after he hanged himself in jail. There were:

- sixteen femurs: six were in pairs, and two were just the left femur
- fifteen medium-sized long bones
- four pairs of elbows
- seven heads of radii (forearms)
- nine lower parts of radii
- eight lower parts of the elbow
- one pair of an upper shinbone
- another pair of a lower elbow with the radii with the extremities still attached
- one pair of upper arms

- one pair of collarbones
- two shoulder blades
- eight heels and ankle bones
- one hundred twenty toes
- sixty-five feet
- one hundred and fifty pieces of ribs

TEN

Carl Grobmann

BERLIN BLUEBEARD

Carl Friedrich Wilhalm Grobmann was born on December 13, 1863, in Neuruppin, Prussia. There isn't much information about Grobmann's childhood, but in his youth, at the age of fifteen, Grobmann was caught sexually assaulting two girls. One was a ten-year-old, who he molested, and the second was a four-year-old, who he raped. The four-year-old died after the assault.

Grobmann was arrested, convicted, and sentenced to fifteen years imprisonment.

When he was released, he went to Berlin. Grohmann had a hot dog stand at a train station close to where he lived. Grohmann also sold other meat to people from his hot dog stand. Several of his customers complained about the meat he was selling. They frequently found pieces of bone in it.

Meanwhile, several women were reported missing in the area, and several body parts were found around Andreas Square and in the Luisenstadt Canal. The coincidence was too much, and quickly, rumours were rife that this was where Grobmann was getting his meat to sell.

On August 21, 1921, after some of Grobmann's neighbors complained to police that they heard loud screaming and banging noises coming from his apartment, the police went to investigate. They arrived at Grobmann's apartment and forced their way in. There, they found a young woman, deceased and tied to his bed. Grobmann was immediately arrested and charged with murder.

Detectives canvassed the neighbors and

learned that Grobmann had often invited females over to his apartment for the last couple of years. The neighbors also told police they would see women entering the apartment, but they usually never saw them leave.

The only body that was ever found was the one police found when they first arrested Grobmann. His apartment was covered with bloodstains on the walls and floors and even on his ceiling. Police were able to determine that the blood belonged to at least three different people, most likely his other victims.

When Grobmann was in jail, and the police were investigating, Grobmann hanged himself in his cell. He was never tried for any murders. However, a police report from 1921 said that Grobmann claimed to have murdered twenty women over twenty years. In the press and public opinion, though, he probably killed upwards of fifty women.

ELEVEN

Fritz Haarmann

BUTCHER OF HANOVER

Friedrich Heinrich Karl "Fritz" Haarmann was born in Hanover, Germany, on October 25, 1879. He was the youngest of six children born to Johanna and Ollie Haarmann. His father was seven years younger than his mother, who was forty-one when they were married. During their marriage, Ollie was gone most of the time as he worked on the road, and during his travels, he had numerous sexual affairs with different women and once even contracted syphilis. Fritz avoided his father as much as possible because he was short-tempered and frequently yelled at the family.

Before Fritz was old enough to attend school, his mother moved him into her bedroom. Due to her health, she was primarily bedridden. During that time, his mother treated him like a little girl. She dressed him in his older sister's hand-me-down clothing and had him play with dolls. She taught him how to sew and clean things.

Fritz started school in 1886, but his teacher often reprimanded him for daydreaming and not paying attention to her lessons. She also noted on his report card that he was spoiled. Fritz's academic record was below average; he wasn't interested in learning anything and didn't like his teachers. He failed twice and had to repeat some school years.

Later, it was discovered that he had been sexually abused by one of his teachers, which might have caused his issues with all of the other teachers and led to his unwillingness to learn.

Fritz quit school in 1894 when he was just

fifteen years old and became an apprentice for a locksmith. Shortly after, he was fired from that job, and he applied to be in the military and was accepted.

Fritz performed well in the military during training. However, within only six months, he started to have memory lapses, and he couldn't remember what he did during those times. Military medical believed that the memory lapses were caused by anxiety, but Fritz blamed it on being in the military and removed himself from service. Fritz returned home and began working with his father, who now owned and operated a cigar factory.

At sixteen, while back home and working, Fritz started luring other boys around his age and sexually assaulting them. In July of 1896, Fritz was arrested for the first time for committing sexual assault on another boy. He was released quickly with no real repercussions. Over the next six months, he continued to get caught for different sexual assaults on other boys, some of them as young as eight years old.

Because of his behavior, in February 1897, he was placed in the Hanover hospital for a psychiatric evaluation. Doctors would certify Fritz as being incurable, deranged, and unfit to be tried for his assaults, so they ordered him to be committed to a mental institute indefinitely.

In January 1898, Fritz's mother visited the institute and helped him escape. He fled to Zurich, Switzerland, staying with a distant relative of his mother's and working as a handyman in a shipyard. Fritz waited for almost two years before he went home to Hanover, hoping the authorities were not still looking for him. He also returned to work for his father at the cigar factory and moved in with his fiancé, Erna Loewert, who eventually became pregnant with his child.

In October 1900, Fritz was called for compulsory military duty. He was deployed to Colmar and trained to become a member of the rifle battalion. He became known as an excellent marksman and had a good reputation in his unit.

A year later, in October 1901, just after his mother had died, Fritz began to experience dizzy spells and even passed out while he was on a military exercise. He was sent to a hospital, where he ended up staying for five months. There, he was diagnosed as unsuitable for military service and discharged. Officially, Fritz was diagnosed with the condition of Dementia Praecox, and because he was discharged for medical reasons, he was given a monthly pension of twenty-one gold marks.

When released from the hospital, Fritz returned to Hanover, moved back in with his wife, and worked at his father's cigar factory. But Fritz and his father's relationship became even more contentious. The frequent confrontations resulted in Fritz quitting his job and suing his father for not making his working conditions suitable for his medical condition.

Fritz's father won the lawsuit, sending Fritz into a panic. He went to his father's house and started a physical fight with him. Fritz's father called the police on him and sued him for assault and making death threats, but the lawsuit was dropped because of a lack of evidence. The court ordered Fritz to have another mental evaluation that diagnosed him as morally inferior and mentally unstable.

Fritz and his fiancé then opened up a fishmongery. About a year into the business, Fritz's fiancé broke off their engagement because she believed he had an affair with another woman. She also fired him from the fishmongery since the business was in her name.

In early 1905, Fritz moved into an apartment and worked occasional odd jobs. He wasn't making enough money to live on, so he started burglarizing other people's homes and stealing from people and stores to survive.

Over the next ten years, Fritz Haarmann served several small sentences for the minor crimes he was caught doing. But in 1913, he was given a five-year sentence after he was caught and arrested during a more serious home robbery. When the police searched his apartment, they found several other items that were reported stolen from various robberies.

When World War I broke out the following year, Germany started compulsory conscription, and most men were sent away to battle. The lack of men available to work left an incredible shortage in the workforce, so they began to allow prisoners, including Haarmann, to work throughout the day and return to the prison at night to sleep. While in prison, Haarmann met several local criminals and set up a good network of people with whom he could trade stolen property.

Even though he had been arrested and jailed for thefts and also been caught having sex with other men, which was illegal at that time, the police established a working relationship with him and made him an official informant. Haarmann used his knowledge of the local criminal activities to become a police informant. He would inform detectives about a planned robbery, for instance. He mainly did this to distract them from him and the illegal things that he was up to.

After the war, Germany was in a terrible depression, and most people were out of work. Many traveled around on trains, going from town to town, looking for work. Police were short-handed and overwhelmed by the higher-than-normal crime rates, making it easier to rationalize allowing someone like Haarmann to work with them. So they assigned him to patrol the Hanover Train Station, where crimes ran rampant. They even gave him a badge to stop and question anybody he needed to. It was a golden opportunity for a person like Fritz Haarmann.

Murders

From 1918 until 1924, Haarmann committed at least twenty-four murders, later believed to have been twenty-seven. His victims were all male and between the ages of ten and twenty-two. At the train station, Haarmann would approach any male coming off the train alone or at the station alone. He would ask to see their traveling papers and start conversing with them.

If he liked the man, he would invite them back to his place for food or maybe offer them a job. Times were so tough that they would willingly go with him. And he did have a badge, so they must have thought it was okay to go with him.

After they arrived at Haarmann's apartment, he would feed them and give them liquor to relax them and make them feel safe. Then he would strike. He would usually kill them by biting their Adam's apple with his teeth, causing them to lose control of their motion and eventually die of asphyxiation. It became known as his "love bite." Haarmann dismembered all of his victim's bodies before he disposed of them. He became proficient and could cut up their body within a few hours.

During this time, Haarmann was selling meat to neighbors and people around his neighborhood. After his arrest, rumors began to circulate that he had used his victim's flesh as the meat supplies for what he was selling to everyone and gained the nickname the "Butcher of Hanover." Detectives would never find any evidence that this was true.

Haarmann dumped the unusable remains and bones of his victims in either the river or a nearby lake. He kept all of the belongings of his victims and either used them, traded them for other stolen property, or sold them to people.

Haarmann had a lover named Hans Grans during this time, who he asserted was involved in all of the murders. Haarmann claimed that Hans would see someone at the train station wearing clothing he liked, like a coat, and ask him if he wanted the clothing. Haarmann would then approach the man, take him home, and murder him for the clothing so he could give it to Hans.

Haarmann's first known murder was of a seventeen-year-old boy, Friedel Rothe, who went missing in late September 1918. Police learned from witnesses that Rothe was last seen at a coffee shop with Haarmann. The detective knew Haarmann from his informant role, so they weren't in any rush to question him about Rothe.

Eventually, they went to Haarmann's apartment only because Rothe's family kept pressuring them to do something about their missing son. When police arrived at the apartment, they found Haarmann in his bed with a naked thirteen-year-old boy. They arrested Haarmann for sexual assault but didn't search the apartment. Haarmann later admitted that when the police were there, Friedel Rothe's head was wrapped in newspaper and hidden behind the stove.

Haarmann was tried and convicted to nine months in prison for the sexual assault, but he avoided serving his sentence for well over a year. The police needed him out in public so that he could keep informing them about different crimes taking place.

Around this time, Haarmann met his lover, Hans Grans, at the train station. Grans had been a runaway living at the station for almost two weeks when Haarmann offered to take him for food and gave him a place to stay. Grans had considered himself heterosexual, but because he needed food, clothing, and money, he did have sex with Haarmann. But Grans never considered Haarmann anything more than a companion. Grans also knew Haarmann was in love with him, so he took advantage of this. Haarmann allowed Grans to continue his relationships with women.

Haarmann eventually served the nine-month prison sentence but was free again by early 1923. He got back together with his lover, Grans, and returned to work for the police, patrolling the Hanover station and being an informant. With everything back in place, Haarmann was now set up to continue his reign of terror over the young men living on the streets of Hanover. His victims were mainly male transients, runaways, and prostitutes, and thanks to his badge, he had easy access to a pool of victims that he could easily lure back to his home.

Haarmann's first murder after that was a seventeen-year-old boy, Fritz Franke, who was a traveling musician, going from town to town, playing piano in restaurants and bars to make a living. The two met at the Hanover Train Station on February 12, 1923, where Haarmann invited the boy back to his apartment for food and drinks. Grans was there with his latest girlfriend and friend when they arrived at his place. They ate and partied late into the night, and according to Grans, he left with the two girls and went to his girlfriend's apartment.

The following day, the two women went to Haarmann's apartment to find Grans. He wasn't there, and Haarmann said Franke had already left for Hamburg. The two women left. Grans later arrived at Haarmann's apartment to find Franke's dead naked body lying on his bed.

Haarmann met another seventeen-year-old boy, Wilhelm Schulze, at the train station five weeks later. Schulze was one of the many young men traveling by train from city to city to find work. Schulze's body was never found, but some of his possessions and clothing were in Haarmann's possession later when he was arrested.

Haarmann murdered two more men in that apartment, sixteen-year-old Ronald Huch and nineteen-year-old Hans Sonnenfeld, and like his previous murder, Haarmann also had the belongings of these two victims in his possession.

In June, Haarmann moved to an attic apartment and continued to murder.

Thirteen-year-old Ernst Ehrenberg was the son of one of his neighbors. Ehrenberg's braces and glasses were later found in Haarmann's apartment.

In August, an eighteen-year-old office clerk, Heinrich Strub, went missing, and many of his possessions were also found in Haarmann's apartment after his arrest.

In September, seventeen-year-old Paul Bronischewski traveled to Bochum to meet his father after finishing a part-time job in Hanover. Police later figured that Bronischewski was at the Hanover Train Station after they found his jacket, pants, and knapsack in Haarmann's apartment.

In October, Haarmann killed seventeen-year-old Richard Graf, who was last seen taking the train to Hanover for some work that he had found. Haarmann committed a second murder in October: sixteen-year-old Wilhelm Erdner, who never returned home from his job. When his family searched for him, witnesses told them they saw the boy with Detective Fritz Honnerbrock–a name Haarmann often used while on patrol at the train station. Haarmann and Grans sold Erdner's bike to a neighbor that same month. A third victim of Haarmann for October was fifteen-year-old Hermann Wolf, who also was last seen at Hanover Train Station on the 24th. Later that same day, another boy went missing from the train station, thirteen-year-old Heinz Brinkmann.

In November, Adolf Hannappel, a seventeen-year-old carpenter's apprentice from Dusseldorf, was last seen traveling to Hanover for a job and never returned. Witnesses reported seeing him sitting on a rather large trunk at the Hanover Train Station and talking to Haarmann and Grans. Another witness claimed to see the three men at a coffee shop later that day.

In December, when he disappeared, nineteen-year-old Adolf Hennies was out looking for a job. None of his remains were ever found, but later, during the trial, Haarmann confessed to dismembering his body.

Haarmann's first murder in 1924 was seventeen-year-old Ernst Spiecker on January 5th. Later, during Haarmann's interrogation, he didn't remember murdering Spiecker but assumed he must have, as he had all of his possessions in his apartment.

Only ten days after Spiecker, Haarmann murdered twenty-year-old Heinrich Koch. It was never uncovered how the two met.

In February, Haarmann killed another two young men, nineteen-year-old Willi Senger and sixteen-year-old Hermann Speichert, two friends who were taking the train into Hanover.

After a short cooling off, Haarmann is believed to have murdered Hermann Bock in April since Bock's possessions were found in Haarmann's apartment. But he was acquitted of Bock's murder at trial as they had no remains or witnesses of the two of them being together.

Sixteen-year-old Alfred Hogrefe ran away from home only one week later and was last seen at Hanover Train Station. Nine days after that, sixteen-year-old Wilhelm Apel, who met Haarmann at the train station, also went missing. Haarmann's last known victim in April was a circus worker, eighteen-year-old Robert Witzel, who was last seen when his mother gave him some money to take the train to Hanover.

Hainz Martin, fourteen years old, left home on May 9th to go to the train station and never returned. Martin's clothing was later found in Haarmann's apartment.

Also in May, a seventeen-year-old salesman, Fritz Wittig, fell victim to Haarmann and Grans. Haarmann later told police that he never had plans to kill Wittig, as he was in the middle of another murder that same day. They killed him because Grans had seen the salesman at the train station, was impressed with the man's suit, and needed a new suit badly. Grans asked Haarmann if he would kill Wittig to have the suit. Haarmann begrudgingly left the body of a ten-year-old boy, Friedrich Abeling, whom he had met while the boy was skipping his school class. He offered him some candy and treats back at Haarmann's apartment.

After completing two murders and dismemberments in one day, Haarmann took two weeks off before going out on patrol again.

On June 5th, Haarmann spotted sixteen-year-old Friedrich Koch walking to college. Koch's friends later testified that Haarmann approached him at trial.

The last known victim of Haarmann was Erich de Vries, a seventeen-year-old whom he met at the Hanover Train Station on June 14th. A few weeks later, de Vries's remains were discovered in a garden at a city park. Haarmann would later tell the court that de Vries was so large that it took him four trips to carry all of his dismembered remains to the park.

On May 17, 1924, two children playing on the Liene River bank discovered a human skull. Detectives started to focus on Haarmann as the possible killer. After the skull was analyzed, it was determined to belong to a man around twenty years old. The first question detectives had to answer was whether this skull was from a recent murder in the city or if it had been dropped there by some grave robbers, a common crime at that time. It was also possible that the skull had been thrown into the river in a different town, as several shared the Liene River.

Before police had a chance to answer questions about the skull, a second one was discovered near where the first one was found. Like the first one, this skull was also identified as belonging to another relatively young male around twenty years of age.

Two weeks later, two more skulls were found

on the Liene River banks and close to where the first two were found. These two skulls belonged to even younger boys, who died when they were still around the preteen ages. With four skulls being found, the township of Hanover came alive with rumors and gossip about what kinds of evil things might be going on there.

After a town meeting, a few hundred residents decided to do a massive search along the whole riverbank of Hanover and a few of the major parks in town. On June 8th, the citizens searched and found many bones, which they brought to the police. What they found alarmed the police enough that they dragged the river that aligned with the downtown part of the city. During their search, police found over five hundred bones, including pieces of human bodies.

After being analyzed by a court doctor, it was determined that they now had pieces of at least twenty-two different human bodies. It was also determined that over half of the remains had recently been discarded into the river. Most of them had knife wounds or cuts on them. It was also determined that about thirty percent belonged to males under thirty.

The fact that Haarmann was previously arrested and convicted of sexually assaulting a thirteen-year-old boy a few years previous moved him to the top of the list of possible suspects by the police. Haarmann knew all of the Hanover police officers and their other informers already, having worked with them for a few years now. To put him under surveillance, they had to hire two officers from the Berlin police department, which began on June 18th.

Four nights later, the undercover officers saw Haarmann arguing with a fourteen-year-old boy at the train station. Haarmann got two police officers to arrest the youth for traveling without the required paperwork.

While at the police station, the boy told officers that he had been staying at Haarmann's apartment for four days, and during that time, he had been raped several times by him. Police immediately returned to Hanover station, arrested Haarmann, and charged him with sexual assault.

After his arrest, police searched Haarmann's apartment, looking for any possible evidence that he might have been involved with any of the body remains they had discovered in the river. Haarmann had only lived in this apartment for just over one year now, so it was alarming for police to find his floors and walls were covered with blood spatter. When they looked through his bedding, it, too, was covered with blood stains. When he was asked about all of the blood that they had found, Haarmann claimed that it was because he had been selling meat illegally to make some money, and the blood came from when he was cutting and wrapping the meat up to sell.

When police canvassed Haarmann's neighbors, they learned that young men and boys visited his apartment quite often, even daily. Quite a few of his neighbors also saw him leaving his house with large sacks full of something. Two of his neighbors claimed to have followed Haarmann. They said he went to the river and emptied whatever was in the sacks he was carrying from the apartment.

Police also found large amounts of clothing stacked in piles throughout the apartment. Figuring that they might have been stolen from his victims, they rounded it all up and brought it to the police station. Police notified anybody who had reported a missing relative or friend over the last two years to see if they wanted them to come to the police station to look at the recovered items and see if they could identify anything.

Every day, people came to the station to identify clothing or items that belonged to their missing relatives. When police confronted

Haarmann with the identified items, he said he had gotten them from trading his used clothing with others.

Confession

On June 29th, the family of Robert Witzel, whose skull was the first one to be discovered on the riverbank, went to the Hanover police station and were able to identify his keys, boots, and all of the clothing that Robert had been wearing on the last day he was seen. When confronted with this evidence, Haarmann broke down and began to confess about the murders he had committed.

During Haarmann's full confession, he claimed that he never once had any intentions of murdering anybody. He claimed that he had a rabid sexual passion that he couldn't control. During sexual relations with other men, he had the uncontrollable urge to bite his Adam's apple in the throes of ecstasy. Before he knew it, the person would collapse and die. He was then forced to dismember their bodies and dispose of them.

Haarmann claimed that he did not like doing this. Quite often, it would make him ill for days afterward. But the passion and heat of the moment was much stronger than the terror of cutting up and disposing of the body.

Haarmann also described in detail his method of taking apart the bodies. He said he always started by drinking a hot cup of black coffee and then laying the body on the floor face up, covering the face with a piece of clothing. Haarmann said he started by cutting open the stomach first, removing the intestines, and placing them in a bucket. Then, he put a towel inside the abdominal cavity before removing anything else because it absorbed most of the blood. Next, he then made three cuts in the rib section, grabbed hold of the ribs, and pushed until they broke away from the shoulders. He then took the heart, lungs, and kidneys from the victim's body, which were placed in the same bucket as the intestines. Next, he severed the arms and legs from the torso and cut as much of the flesh from them as he could. The flesh was usually flushed down the toilet. One of the last things he would do was to cut the head from the body. He used a smaller knife to remove the flesh from the head and face and the back end of his axe to smash the skull until it split. The brains were removed and placed in his bucket.

Haarmann dumped all the bones and remains from the bucket into the Liene River. He also argued that the skulls the police found were not from his victims, as he always split the skull open to remove the brains, and none of the skulls they discovered were split open.

When the detectives asked Haarmann how many people he killed, Haarmann told them it was somewhere between fifty and seventy, but he couldn't be sure as he lost count.

Police could only connect Haarmann with twenty-seven of the missing men with the evidence they had. By July 8th, they were able to formally charge Haarmann with the twenty-seven murders and charge his lover Grans with accessory to one murder. Both Haarmann and Grans were given a mental examination, and both were found fit to stand trial.

Trial

On December 4, 1924, the trial for both Haarmann and Grans began. Haarmann was charged with twenty-seven murders between the dates of September 1918 and June 1924. Haarmann admitted to fourteen of the murders that he was charged with. Grans was charged with being an accessory to murder in most of these cases, and he pleaded not guilty on all counts.

The court initially allowed spectators to the trial, but given the gruesome details, the judge excluded spectators by day three. The trial lasted about two weeks, with one hundred ninety witnesses taking the stand and over one thousand pieces of evidence.

On December 19, 1924, Haarmann was convicted of twenty-four of the twenty-seven murders he was charged with. After the floor person read the verdict, Haarmann stood up proudly and said that he was going to be beheaded happily. Whereas, Grans cried out loud and became hysterical when the floor man read out that he, too, was guilty of inciting murder and sentenced to death as well by beheading plus an additional twelve years of imprisonment.

Haarmann would file no appeal on his convictions or the sentence; he felt that he would continue to kill if he was allowed to live. On the other hand, Grans filed an appeal of his conviction and sentence, but it was denied the following year.

Execution

Fritz Haarmann was executed on April 15, 1925, by guillotine on the grounds of the Hanover prison. He was given his final wishes of smoking an expensive cigar, having a cup of Brazilian coffee, and having a pastor prayer over him. Only selected members were allowed to watch Haarmann's execution without any of the press there.

Aftermath

After the execution of Haarmann, sections of his brain had been removed for science to analyze. The only thing that was found was that he had traces of meningitis. Haarmann's head was then preserved in formaldehyde and remained in possession of Gottingen Medical School until 2014, when it was cremated.

Grans' Retrial

Soon after Haarmann was executed, Grans' father came forward to the court and gave them a letter he claimed was written by Haarmann, dated February 5, 1925. The letter stated that Haarmann wrote that Grans had no idea that he had been killing men. Haarmann was only frustrated and upset that Grans was only using him and didn't love him. And that was the reason

Haarmann said that Grans was involved. He also claimed in the letter that he said it because he was under extreme pressure from the police during their interrogations.

In January 1926, Hans Grans was given a retrial based on the letter. Grans was again found guilty of aiding and abetting in two of the murders that Haarmann was convicted of doing. This time, however, his sentence wasn't death. Instead, he received two twelve-year sentences to be served in prison concurrently.

After Grans completed his twelve-year sentence, he was sent to Sachsenhausen and placed in a concentration camp, where he would remain until the war ended in April 1945. After that, he lived in Hanover as a free man until he died in 1975.

TWELVE

Joachim Kroll

MAN EATER

J oachim Kroll was born in Hindenburg, Germany on April 17, 1933. He was the sixth of nine children. His father was a miner, but when the war broke out, his father was sent off to fight and would be captured during a battle and held as a prisoner of war. After that, the family moved to North Rhine-Westphalia to stay with his mother's family.

In 1955, when Kroll was twenty-two, and after his mother died, he moved to Duisburg to work as a washroom attendant. Within a year, he got a much better job working for Thyssen Industries, a steel manufacturer. It was also around this time that he started his gruesome killing spree of women and girls.

Kroll was very precise about how he killed his victims. He often followed them around for a while, and when they were in a place where nobody else was around, he would approach them and, without saying a word, grab his victim by the neck with both hands and strangle them until they were dead. Kroll would remove their clothing and have intercourse with their body and sometimes masturbate afterward while standing over them. Kroll would then cut off some of their body parts or flesh to take back to his apartment so that he could eat it later.

Back at his apartment, a few neighbors noticed their pipes backing up almost daily. When one of Kroll's neighbors approached him to ask if he was also having this problem, he said it was probably just the human guts getting stuck.

This neighbor decided to tell the police what

Kroll said. Police went to Kroll's apartment to question him, and once they arrived, they found the remains of a female victim who was cut up into several small pieces in his living room. Kroll was arrested immediately.

During their interrogation of Kroll, he admitted to murdering thirteen women and trying to kill another woman, but she escaped. He also gave significant details about how he killed them and that he used to cut off different body parts and flesh from their bodies to take home and eat later. He was proud that he could save money on his grocery bills by doing this.

Kroll thought that instead of going to prison, he would be castrated and let go. At that time, that was often the punishment for sexual predators. Instead, the court decided to charge and convict him with eight murders and one attempted murder. After a hundred and fifty-day trial in April 1982, he was sentenced to a term of life imprisonment. Nine years later, in 1991, Kroll died of a heart attack in his cell.

THIRTEEN

Paul Ogorzow

S-BAHN MURDERER

P aul Ogorzow, born Paul Saga, was born in Muntowen, East Prussia, on September 29, 1912. Today, it is known as Muntowo, Poland. His single mother raised him until he was twelve. After she married Johann Ogorzow, who would later adopt Paul, he changed his name to Paul Ogorzow.

When Ogorzow turned eighteen years old, he joined the Nazi party, and he eventually became part of their paramilitary branch that carried out jobs the regular military and police wouldn't do. In 1933 when the Nazis gained power, Ogorzow became the squad leader or SA of his troop. The following year, he was hired as a trackman for the National Railroad or Deutsche Reichsbahn and ran the S-Bahn commuter rail system in Berlin. Eventually, he became the signalman at the Rummelsberg depot in eastern Berlin.

In 1937, Ogorzow married Gertrude Ziegelmann, who was two years older than him, and they had two children. Later, during his trial, she testified against him, telling the court that he was often violent, had loud outbursts, and frequently accused her of being unfaithful to him.

Meanwhile, his work gave him lots of praise, and he was well-liked and considered very good at his job. Ogorzow was a reliable supervisor and always wore a clean and well-pressed uniform anywhere he was dispatched.

Ogorzow's first attack was thought to have been in the Summer of 1939. At that time, he was living with his family in Karlshorst. Initially, the police had no idea who was behind the random attack, but later, after his arrest, Ogorzow admitted to what he did. Ogorzow went to the Friedrichsfelde district of Berlin – an area with mainly homemakers and children living alone, as their husbands had been called away to fight in the war – to look for victims. In 1939, the police documented thirty-one attacks in that area where the women were threatened with a knife, choked, and sometimes raped by their assailant. Every one of the victims told officers that their attacker wore a railway uniform. Later, all thirty-one of these assaults would be connected to Ogorzow.

Ogorzow's last victim in 1939 was a woman who he thought was traveling alone. After he began to try to assault her sexually, she began to scream, and her husband and brother-in-law came running from another car. He barely escaped but, in the process, got beaten up badly.

The following year, in 1940, Ogorzow began making precise plans on how to find his victims without getting caught and started to attack women on the train again. In Berlin, during the war, none of the train cars were lit up while traveling, and he would hang around in the empty cars waiting for females traveling alone to enter.

Ogorzow, wearing his railway worker's

uniform, approached the travelers to ask for their tickets. None of the travelers were scared of a railway worker wearing a uniform, so they would comply with his requests. While they were looking for their ticket in the purse, he attacked, striking them several times with a two-inch thick piece of lead-encased telephone cable that he carried.

His first known murder victim was twenty-year-old Gerda Ditter, whose husband was away fighting in the war. Once Ogorzow got her alone in a car on the train, he raped her and then stabbed her to death. Ogorzow raped and killed several other women who were riding on the train. He would catch them unawares and hit, strangle, or stab them until they were dead. Afterward, he would throw them from the moving train.

Even though the police were aware of all of the sexual assaults and murders taking place, none of them were reported to the press. The Nazi Propaganda Minister didn't want this kind of news out to the public, so they didn't put out a warning to lone travelers, and they controlled everything that was reported. This policy made it so the detectives couldn't canvas or ask questions of any possible witnesses.

Police sent out their best detectives to discreetly try to investigate the attacks. They started by interviewing five thousand Berlin railway workers. They also sent undercover officers to ride the trains and watch all female riders. They sent out undercover policewomen as decoys to try and catch the killer. Ogorzow noticed the increased police presence and questioning of railway workers, making him very cautious and almost inactive for the first five months of 1941. When he began to attack again, it wasn't done on the train or to any passengers.

Eventually, police singled out Ogorzow and started concentrating on him after receiving abnormal reports from railway employees. Quite often, he would tell other workers how fascinated he was with murder, and he would make misogynist comments about the female passengers. Detectives asked Ogorzow to come in for an interview, and while he was there, they noticed blood stains on his uniform, which gave them enough cause to place him under arrest.

During his interrogation, detectives brought in one of his victims to face him directly. They also brought in a tray containing several pieces of skulls and other things from some of his other victims. Ogorzow confessed.

Ogorzow tried to claim that the cause of his attacks and murder of women was due to his severe alcoholism and that a Jewish doctor had not treated him correctly for a gonorrhea infection that he had. The prosecutor on the case proposed that Ogorzow had an excessive sex drive, was sexually attracted to his victims' resistance, and had a deep hatred of women.

Ogorzow was expelled from the Nazi party and declared an enemy of the people. He pled guilty to eight murders, six attempted murders, and thirty-one cases of sexual assault. He was sentenced to death on July 24, 1941, and two days later, was executed by guillotine at the Plotzensee Prison.

FOURTEEN

Rudolf Pleil

THE DEATHMAKER

Rudolf Pleil was born on July 7, 1924, in Germany near the border to the former Czechoslovakia, which was under communist rule until the Nazi movement took over in 1938. Within a year of the Nazi occupation, Pleil's father was arrested and taken away. Rudolf had been doing odd jobs since he was nine years old, but after his father was taken, he was under pressure to support his whole family, so he quit school.

At a young age, Pleil was dabbling in petty crimes and smuggling illegal contraband over the old border. These petty crimes caused him to be arrested several times, but he served no jail time as he was still a minor.

Pleil left his home at fifteen and started working as a barge ship boy. He continued his illegal activities, including smuggling. In 1933, he applied and got accepted to the Nazi navy but was quickly dismissed when they discovered he had epilepsy.

In 1945, when the Russian Red Army invaded the area, he began working as a police officer for the Russians. Along with twelve others, he patrolled the border with groups since so many officers had been killed at the border region during that time.

His illegal smuggling activity continued. He and his two duty partners, Karl Hoffmann and Konrad Schubler, started smuggling people, mainly women, who had money, from East Germany to West Germany. Pleil and his two duty partners also began to rob, rape, and murder some of the women they came across at the border. They would all use various weapons, such as hatchets, knives, hammers, and even rocks, to kill their victims.

Several women, at least twelve, were found to have been attacked and murdered over the two years of 1946 to 1947. Because of the considerable unrest from the war, the police could not spend much time on the crimes happening in that area.

In 1947, Pleil got into an argument with a businessman, Hermann Bennen, at the border, and it quickly became physical. Pleil grabbed a hatchet and killed Bennen. He was arrested and charged only with manslaughter as he was extremely drunk at the time of the murder. The court gave him a twelve-year prison sentence.

While Pleil was in custody for the Bennen killing, a woman who had been attacked previously by Pleil felt safe enough to go to the police to tell them about her encounter with him. The detectives took her information and began to investigate other female victims of the border region from 1946 to 1947 to see if Pleil could have been involved in those murders.

Eventually, Pleil confessed to many of the

rapes and murders that he was accused of. He also told detectives about his two accomplices in many of them. By February 18, 1958, his two accomplices were charged with several crimes, including theft, rape, and murder.

In October 1950, the trial began for all three of the accused murderers. The *German Press* and several international media covered the entire trial. Pleil loved the attention he was getting and talked to reporters openly all the time. He would greatly exaggerate the crimes that he had committed.

Pleil's defense was that he had a mental illness and, therefore, should be sent to a hospital to be treated rather than to be sent to prison. His defense was unsuccessful, and on November 17, 1950, the court sentenced Pleil and both of his accomplices to life imprisonment for nine of the murders.

While Pleil was in custody, he confessed to several more of the murders that happened in the area. He also wrote his memoir, *Mein Kampf,* in honor of Adolf Hitler. In his memoir, he claimed to have murdered at least twenty-five different women, bragging that he had killed one more than Fritz Haarmann. He called himself the "greatest murderer ever."

On February 16, 1958, Pleil hanged himself in his cell. As for his two accomplices, Karl Hoffmann died in prison, and Konrad Schubler was released early in 1970.

Known Victims

1946

1. Erica M.: thirty-two years old, robbed, raped, and murdered by heavy blows to her head.
2. Unknown Female: approximately twenty-five years old; July 19th; Pleil admitted to sexually assaulting her and then killing her with a hammer; her body was recovered but remains unidentified.
3. Unknown Female: twenty-five years old; August 19th; both Pleil and Karl Hoffmann lured her to a private location where they both raped her; Hoffmann stabbed her in the head afterward; her body was recovered in 1946 and remains unidentified.
4. Inga X: twenty-five years old; September 2nd; crossing the border

when Pleil robbed her and killed her by hitting her on the head with a rock; her body was discovered in September.

5. Frau X: twenty-five years old; crossing the border when stopped by Pleil; both Pleil and Hoffman robbed her; Hoffman raped her and killed her by cutting her head off; her body was discovered in November.

6. Krista 3: twenty-five years old; mid-September; met Pleil at the border, and he offered to guide her to where she was going; while in the forest, Pleil claimed to have had an epileptic seizure and passed out; when he woke, the woman was dead, and her body was lying on the ground beside him; her body was discovered a few days after her death.

7. Unknown Female: fifty-five years old; December 12th; robbed and beaten unconscious with clubs by both Pleil and Schubler; they left her body covered by branches in the woods, but she was not dead; when she regained consciousness, she went to the police

and later became an important witness at their trial.
8. Unknown Female: thirty-seven years old; December 14th; Pleil killed her at the border crossing in front of Schubler; he threw her body down a well.
9. Unknown Female: forty-four years old; December 19th; Pleil killed her and threw her body down the same well.

1947

1. Margot M: twenty years old; January 16th; Pleil and Hoffman asked her to go to dinner with them; after they ate and on their way back to the border, Pleil murdered her and dumped her body in a creek; her remains were discovered the following day.
2. Frau S.: forty-nine years old; raped and beaten to death with an iron rod; Hoffmann robbed her and piled a stack of chopped wood on top of her corpse; her body was found a week later.

3. Unknown Woman: March; Pleil and Hoffmann murdered her by stabbing her to death; Hoffmann cut off her head; her head was discovered a week later, and her body was found quite a distance away a few more weeks later.

FIFTEEN

Jürgen Bartsch

THE CARNIVAL KILLER

Jürgen Bartsch was born Karl-Heinz Sadrozinski on November 6, 1946. He didn't know his father, and his mother died of tuberculosis when he was only six months old. He was cared for by nurses until he reached eleven months old when he was adopted by a butcher and his wife from Langenberg.

His adoptive mother had OCD and was obsessed with cleanliness. She wouldn't allow him to play with other kids for fear that he would get dirty. He was placed in a Catholic school as his mother didn't think regular school was strict enough. Her fixation on cleanliness led her to continue bathing him herself until he was nineteen years old.

Jürgen was abused by his mother his whole life. She not only sexually abused him during his bath time but would often beat him in the butcher shop and in front of anyone who was around. Jürgen was also abused by a teacher in school when he was thirteen years old, as well as a distant cousin often forced him to have sex with him when he was only eight years old.

In 1962, at the age of fifteen, Jürgen began to kill. He would lure his intended victim to an abandoned air raid shelter, and once inside, he made them take their clothes off, and he sexually assaulted them. After that, he killed them and dismembered their bodies.

His first four victims were eight-year-old Klaus Jung in 1962, thirteen-year-old Peter Fuchs in 1965, twelve-year-old Ulrich Kahlweiss also in

1965, and twelve-year-old Manfred Grassmann in 1966.

His fifth victim, fifteen-year-old Peter Frese, had escaped and survived the assault also in 1966. Like his previous four victims, Jürgen brought Frese to the air raid shelter and forced him to undress before sexually assaulting him. He enjoyed Frese so much that he wanted to keep him alive to return and assault him again. Jürgen left Frese tied up and left a candle burning for him when he left to go home. While he was gone, Frese managed to burn his binding with the candle and escaped. After getting home, Frese reported his assault to the police.

Jürgen was arrested and charged by the police. During his interrogation, he confessed to all his crimes without hesitation. He was convicted and given a life sentence on December 15, 1967.

In 1971, an appeal was granted, which reduced his prison sentence to ten years in a juvenile facility where he would be placed under psychiatric care. While there, he met and married Gisela Deike on January 2, 1974.

During his time in the psychiatric facility, it was suggested by doctors that Jürgen be either castrated or undergo some psychosurgery as a treatment to alleviate his problems. Jürgen refused any surgery for the first few years. On April 28, 1976, he agreed to a voluntary castration to be released from the mental hospital sometime in the future once the doctors felt it was safe. During the castration process, Jürgen died of an accidental overdose of halothane, the drug used as anesthesia for the surgery.

SIXTEEN

Heinrich Pommerenke

THE BEAST OF THE BLACK FOREST

Heinrich Max Pommerenke was born on July 6, 1937, in Bentwisch, Germany. Heinrich lived with his grandparents in Mecklenburg as his father died while fighting in World War II, and his mother left for Switzerland after the war.

While he was still in school, he committed his first rape. He sexually assaulted a girl but wasn't arrested. After he finished his schooling in 1953 and became an apprentice as a painter, he committed another rape and fled to West Berlin. He was later arrested and sent to live with his mother and sister in Switzerland.

While living with his mother, Pommerenke got a job working at a fair, helping clean the grounds. Soon after, he was again accused of rape, and the Swiss authorities kicked him out of the country and banned him from entering again for ten years. He returned to Germany.

Pommerenke started his murderous spree in 1959. According to his confession, it was triggered by watching *The Ten Commandments* at a movie theater in February of that year. From that movie, he decided that women were the root of all evil, and his mission was to punish them. That same night, Pommerenke committed his first murder in a nearby park. He raped and slit the throat of forty-nine-year-old Hilde Konter and left her at the highway junction in Durlach.

The following month he kidnapped an eighteen-year-old girl and brought her to his cabin on the outskirts of Hornberg, where he raped her, beat her, and finally killed her by hitting her on her head with a large rock. He threw her body in a river, which was discovered a week later on the banks of a nearby town.

On May 30th, Pommerenke broke through a window of an eighteen-year-old girl's bedroom and tried to rape her. She was able to break free and scream for help. He fled the house when he heard her father coming down the stairs. The victim was able to give a good description of her attacker to the police.

The next day, Pommerenke boarded a tourist train from the central railway station in Heidelberg just before midnight. While on the train, he stabbed twenty-one-year-old Dagmar Klimek to death and threw her body off the train. Quickly, he pressed the emergency brake, and when the train came to a stop, he got off to find her body. He found her body a couple of miles away from where the train had stopped. He dragged her corpse to a gravel road and had sex with it.

The day after, when the train reached its stop and Dagmar wasn't on it, she was reported missing to the train authorities by her friends. It wasn't long before they connected the missing person to the unusual emergency brake stop. When they questioned other passengers, two witnesses reported seeing a man leave the train when it had stopped. Her body was discovered on June 5th.

Three days before Dagmar's body was discovered, Pommerenke attacked a waitress with an ironbound wood and stole her purse near a train station. A few days later, Pommerenke decided to ride his bike around Karlsruhe looking for victims. He ended up stabbing two women in the neck, severely injuring them.

Pommerenke was now dubbed the "Beast of the Black Forest" for his reign of terror over the residents of Baden-Württemberg.

Pommerenke's next attack was on a fifteen-year-old girl. On June 8th, he broke into her house through a window and stabbed her in the neck. The attack was heard and interrupted by her father, and he fled. Police were able to get his foot imprint from the sole of his boots from just outside of the house.

The following day, June 9th, Pommerenke raped and strangled sixteen-year-old Rita Walterspacher, close to Baden-Baden, and dumped her body in the forest just outside of town. The day after that, on June 10th,

Pommerenke broke into a gun shop in Baden-Baden and stole a small caliber rifle and an air-pressure pistol.

A week later, he broke into a railway station's ticket office and robbed them of 540 deutchemarks. He got away without any good witness descriptions. That same day, he picked up a tailor-made suit he had ordered and paid for beforehand. He ordered it under his real name.

The police also got a footprint from the train station robbery, which matched the footprint from the attack on June 8th, tying them together.

On June 19th, a man found Pommerenke's old clothing and his air gun, which he had left hidden, and gave it to the police. On that same day, a detective spotted Pommerenke at a train station and thought he looked like the description of the attacker given by one of the girls. He arrested him and took him back to the police station for questioning.

During his interrogation, Pommerenke confessed to sixty-five offenses, consisting of four murders, seven attempted murders, two rapes, twenty-five attempted rapes, six robberies, ten burglaries, and six thefts.

Pommerenke's trial started on October 3, 1960, and the court decided not to prosecute thirty-eight of his offenses as they all took place before he was twenty-one. But he ended up being convicted on all other counts and, on October 22nd, received six life imprisonment sentences and another fifteen years. This sentence was the highest amount of years sentenced to one prisoner in West Germany since World War II ended.

Pommerenke died on December 27, 2008, from leukemia in Hohenasperg at seventy-one years old. He was cremated and his ashes scattered in the sea. At the time of his death, he was Germany's longest-serving prisoner ever.

SEVENTEEN

Olaf Däter

THE GRANNY KILLER

Olaf Däter was born on September 25, 1969, in Bremerhaven, West Germany. His mother was not married to his father and was, therefore, regarded as "illegitimate." His stepfather later adopted him, and he grew up as an only child in his home.

After Däter finished school, he joined the military and worked as a nurse in their medical services unit. While working as an army nurse, Däter married another nurse working for the same unit, but they divorced within one year.

After his military career was over, Däter was able to become a nurse. He enjoyed working with elderly patients and worked as a gerontological nurse.

In early 2001, Däter began dating a sex worker he liked and wanted to impress. He would take her out for expensive dinners and rent luxurious cars to drive her around. Däter was putting himself in significant debt from these expenses. Around the same time, Däter lost his job as a nurse and was heavily in debt.

Suddenly, several of Däter's previous elderly female patients died. At first, their deaths were presumed to be because of their ages, but something more nefarious was at play.

One of the patient's sons decided to check on his mother at her home. When he called, instead of his mother answering the phone, a man answered and hung up immediately. The son called the police, told them what had happened, and immediately left for his mother's place. He arrived just as the police got there.

When they entered her place, they found his mother lying on the floor of the living room unconscious. When she woke up, she told them all that it was her previous nurse, Däter, who had come to her home and attacked her. Detectives then found out that another of his patients had been murdered in her home earlier that day.

Detectives put a warrant out for Däter's arrest and found him outside his parent's home. Before Däter could get to the front door, the police arrested him while both of his parents watched.

During his interrogation, Däter admitted to murdering four other of his patients earlier that month. His victims had been his patients when he was their nurse, so they all knew him and trusted him. They let him in without hesitation when he came to their door.

During his visit with the women, he attacked them from behind when they weren't expecting anything. He suffocated them, covering their mouths and then pushing them onto the floor. Däter was seriously overweight, and he used his weight to his advantage. He placed his knee on their back and then laid his whole body over theirs until they died. Däter stole any cash he could find but left their jewelry and other valuables.

The police did not know about Däter's four

other victims until he confessed. They were initially ruled as natural deaths since there were no signs of an attack. Because all of the jewelry and valuables were left behind, their deaths weren't suspicious.

Detectives also discovered that Däter had not left his last nursing job, as he said. Apparently, he had been caught stealing from the patients he was taking care of and fired. It was revealed that the same happened with his nursing position in the military as well. The military kept his file sealed until the police investigated the murders.

Däter was sentenced to life imprisonment at Landgericht Bremen, and his motive was financial. His debt was in the five figures by the time of his arrest. Däter also admitted that he would have kept on doing the murders for the money if he had not been caught.

EIGHTEEN

Fritz Honka

HAMBURG'S REDLIGHT KILLER

F ritz Honka was born in Leipzig, Germany, on July 31, 1935, and was the third in a line of ten children. His father was a boilerman who was sent to a concentration camp because it was believed he had worked for the communists and died by 1946. His mother was a house cleaner, unable to manage nine children without a husband, so Fritz grew up in a children's home.

Sometime in the early 1950s, Fritz became an apprentice bricklayer but quickly developed an allergy and had to quit. After that, Fritz headed to West Germany and worked as a farmhand in Brockofe. During his time on the farm, he had an affair with a woman named Margot, and they had a child. This embarrassed him to leave the town after paying her three thousand Deutschmark alimony.

Fritz ended up in Hamburg, where he got a job working on the harbor front, married, and had another son named Fritz. The marriage didn't last a year as Fritz and his wife had loud, violent fights where even the neighbors got involved. They separated in 1967.

Fritz moved in with another woman named Irmgard Albrecht in the Summer of 1972. In August of that same year, he met Ruth Dufner and invited her to his house for dinner. After they ate, Fritz tried to force Ruth to have sex with both him and his wife. She managed to escape undressed and ran to the local police station to report the assault. Ruth needed minor treatment at the hospital for some cuts and bruises.

In April 1975, the court dropped the charges

of rape on Fritz as he had a high blood alcohol level at the time of the assault but ordered him to pay a 4500 Deutschmarks fine.

Murders

The first murder that Fritz was known to have committed was in December 1970. At that time, Fritz worked as the night watchman on the waterfront. A local hairdresser, Gertraud Brauer, who was forty-two, always walked by him on her way home from work. Fritz would often flirt with her and ask her to go out with him or, sometimes, try to get her in an alley to have sex with him, but she would always refuse. Finally, one night in late December, Fritz got angry with her and strangled her to death. To cover his crime, he sawed up her remains into smaller pieces, wrapped in paper, and hid them in different places around the harbor.

 Hamburg police eventually found some of the wrapped body parts and were able to identify whose body it was, but they were never able to find the killer. The murder was not solved until years later when Fritz confessed.

 The next known murder was four years later, in August 1974. He picked up a fifty-four-year-old sex worker, Anna Beuschel, and brought her to his apartment. While they were having sex, Fritz decided to strangle her because, as he later said, she wasn't passionate enough. Fritz went on to murder two more sex workers, fifty-seven-year-old Frieda Roblick in December 1974 and fifty-two-year-old Ruth Schult, in January 1975, in the same way and for the same reason.

Just like when Fritz first murdered his first victim, Gertraud Brauer, he also cut up the body remains of the other three sex workers and wrapped them in paper. These body parts he hid in his attic so that no one would find them.

It wasn't long before other tenants living in the same building began complaining about the foul odor, so Fritz used pine-scented perfume blocks to cover the smell.

Fritz was in a minor car accident when he first moved to Hamburg, which left a permanent mark on his nose and caused a problem with his speech. Physically, Fritz had a slight build, standing only five foot six inches and only one hundred and forty pounds.

Quite often, he would get drunk before hiring a sex worker, and he would let out his anger on them. He would always get a sex worker who was shorter than him, and he preferred ones without teeth so that they couldn't mutilate his genitals during sex with him.

In July 1975, Fritz's apartment building caught on fire. When the firefighters arrived to put out the blaze, they found partially decomposing female body parts in the attic. The police were called, and they searched the apartment building. They found a plastic bag with a woman's torso in it. When Fritz came home after work that day, the police arrested him.

Within a week, Fritz confessed to murdering the three women and cutting up their bodies. One year later, in November, Fritz withdrew his confession, claiming now that he remembered nothing at all about the women.

Fritz was found guilty of one count of murder and three counts of manslaughter and sentenced to fifteen years in prison at a psychiatric hospital. The court considered his chronic use of alcohol diminished his mental capacity.

In 1993, Fritz was released, and his name was changed to Peter Jensen. He spent the next five years, until his death, in a nursing home in Langenhorn, Hamburg.

NINETEEN

Erwin Hagedorn

EAST GERMAN BLOODLUST MURDERER

Erwin Hagedorn was born on January 30, 1952, in Eberswalde, Brandenburg, East Germany. He was the last criminal in Germany to be executed, although later, there were some politically motivated criminals executed.

When Hagedorn was only seventeen years old, he began killing. On May 31, 1969, in a park located in Eberswalde, he attacked two nine-year-old boys with a knife. Both victims died from deep wounds to their necks, and one of the boys was cut so viciously that his head was severed from his body. Their remains were found about two weeks after their murders. Detectives were focused on known child murderers in the area, so Hagedorn was not suspected at the time.

Over a year later, Hagedorn struck again. On October 7, 1971, twelve-year-old Ronald Winkler was walking in the same park where Hagedorn killed his first two victims. Winkler was knifed to death just as severely as the other two victims had been. During the investigation, they learned that he had been sexually harassed by Erwin Hagedorn just before his murder. A month later, on November 12, 1971, police arrested Hagedorn and charged him with all three murders.

In the early Summer of 1972, Hagedorn was convicted of all three murders as well as sexual abuse and attempted sexual abuse. Since East Germany had abolished the death penalty for minors, he only received the death penalty for the murder of Winkler. After an appeal was rejected, the then-twenty-year-old Hagedorn was executed by a single shot to the back of the neck on September 15, 1972. Hagedorn was then cremated, and the ashes were buried in a secret place so that they would not be damaged.

TWENTY

Volker Eckert

THE TRUCKDRIVER KILLER

Volker Eckert was born on July 1, 1959, in Plauen, Germany. Sometime in the 1960s, his mother threw his father out of their apartment, where Volker lived with two other siblings.

When Volker was around the age of nine, he found himself sexually aroused whenever he touched the hair on any of his sister's dolls. The sensation led Volker to play with his mother's wigs, which were more life-size and had longer hair, arousing him even more.

Volker was shy about his fantasies and didn't tell anyone else as he was scared that they would make fun of him. Wanting to take his arousal further, he ended up getting some of his own dolls to play with. Volker didn't think any real woman would let him touch their hair. Not for the reasons he had.

Murders

When Volker was only fourteen years old, in 1974, he made his first kill. One afternoon, he lured one of his classmates, Silvia Unterdorfel, into her attic. Once in the attic, Volker tried to stroke and caress her hair, and when she resisted, he strangled her to death. He then spent time playing with her hair.

Once Volker had fulfilled his fantasy, he took a skipping rope and wrapped it around her neck, tying the other end to a door knob to make it appear as if she had killed herself. When Silvia's body was discovered, police ruled it a suicide, and the case was closed. The truth wasn't known until thirty-two years later when Volker revealed his secret.

A year later, Volker got a job working with his estranged father as a painter, which gave him more freedom away from his home and a reason to be out on the streets. In 1977, Volker was caught sexually assaulting and strangling a woman he had met while walking home from his job. Volker served an eight-month sentence for this crime and was released when he turned nineteen.

Between the years when Volker was released from prison in 1979 and 1987, he began assaulting as many as thirty different women on the dark streets of his town. Often, during the attack, Volker choked the victims until they passed out, but he didn't kill them.

In 1987, a murdered woman was found in the woods of Plauen. Eighteen-year-old Heike Wunderlich had been raped and strangled. Detectives ruled out Volker since the victim had been raped, and that was not something Volker had done before. The case eventually went cold, giving Volker more confidence to continue.

Near the end of 1987, a sixteen-year-old girl, Claudia, was walking home alone when Volker spotted her. He began to follow her, trying to keep her from noticing him. As soon as she was walked down a private alley, he approached her and attacked her. Volker strangled her so that he could stroke her hair. Once he was finished, he went home. Claudia regained consciousness and was able to describe her assailant to the police. They created a composite sketch to hand out to the public, and it wasn't long before Volker was recognized and arrested.

In 1988, Volker was charged with attempted murder of Claudia and convicted to spend twelve years in prison. He was released in July 1994 after just six years in prison. He didn't get into any trouble with the law for the next five years.

In 1999, Volker became a truck driver, traveling all around Europe. It wasn't long before it was noticed that many women, many of them sex workers, were missing or found raped and murdered throughout Europe in 2001. But it wasn't until police saw footage caught by a surveillance camera in November 2006 of Volker's truck in a parking lot with a naked corpse lying on the ground beside it that police detained Volker for questioning.

During their interrogation, Volker confessed to

six murders, including that of his classmate Silvia Unterdorfel. The others included:

1. A Nigerian sex worker found in Bordeaux, France, on June 21, 2001
2. A twenty-four-year-old sex worker found in Catalonia, Spain, on October 9, 2001
3. A Russian Sex worker was found in Catalonia, Spain, on March 1, 2006
4. A twenty-eight-year-old Polish sex worker found in Reims, France
5. A twenty-year-old Bulgarian Sex worker found in Hostalric, Spain, on November 2, 2006

Volker wouldn't confess to these murders, and there wasn't enough evidence to charge him, but detectives on the case also suspected him of seven other murders:

1. Eighteen-year-old girl found in Plauen, Germany, in April 1987
2. Twenty-three-year-old sex worker from Sierre Leone found in Troyes, France, in August 2022

3. Twenty-five-year-old sex worker from Ghana found in Rezzato, Italy, on September 5, 2004
4. Three other unidentified women found in the Czech Republic, and one other woman found in France

His trial began on July 1, 2007, and after the first day of trial was completed, Volker was taken back to his cell. He killed himself in his cell before the second day of his trial could begin.

TWENTY-ONE

Norbert Hans Poehlke
THE HAMMER KILLER

Norbert Hans Poehlke was born on September 15, 1951, and died on October 22, 1985, in a murder-suicide.

Norbert first became a police officer in 1971 in Baden-Wurttemberg and worked his way up to being the sergeant of the canine division. He was married and had three children, two boys and a girl.

In 1982, Norbert won 36,000 Deutschmarks from the lottery and built a new house for his family in Strumpfelbach. Unfortunately, he overspent on the new house and went into debt. More bad news came to the family in March 1984 when his daughter died of a brain tumor when she was only three years old.

A few months later, a series of robberies and murders began to happen in the area. People and banks were targeted, and all had the same pattern. The victim was lured to their car and got in with the perpetrator. They were robbed of money and valuables and then shot in the head. The victim's body was placed in the vehicle's trunk, and then the killer used the victim's vehicle in a bank robbery.

The robber-killer would eventually be dubbed the "Hammer Killer," as he was masked when he entered the bank and carried a sledgehammer. He smashed the windows of the bank tellers before robbing their drawers of cash, exiting the bank, and leaving the murdered victim and their car behind in the bank parking lot.

Murders

On May 3, 1984, Siegfried Pfitzer, forty-seven years old engineer, was found shot in the head at a rest stop in Marbach, West Germany. His car was used in a bank robbery. Later, it was found about a quarter of a mile from the rest stop where his body was found.

Thirty-seven-year-old Englishman Eugene Wethey, living in Germany, was found shot to death on December 21, 1984, at a different rest stop near Grossbottwar. On December 26th, Wethey's car was used in a bank robbery in Cleebronn by the "Hammer Killer."

About six months later, on July 22, 1985, twenty-six-year-old Wilfried Scheider was found shot to death in a parking lot in Beilstein-Schmidhausen. His car was also used at a bank robbery in Spiegelberg.

After that, the police set up a task force and went to the media to ask for help from the public. Their plea for help led to five hundred and forty clues and interviews of over fourteen hundred people.

During a police search of a train station in Ludwigsburg, a police uniform was found in a locker. The uniform was traced to Norbert

Poehlke. When asked why his uniform was left at a train station locker, he told them it was because he had to change his clothes quickly to go to a family funeral. On further investigation, police discovered that Norbert had not attended any funerals since the one for his daughter in 1984.

A month later, Norbert requested and was given some time off for sick leave. On October 14th, detectives went to Norbert's home to question him again, but there was no answer. Police began to think that Norbert decided to go on the run, so they broke into his house. There, they found Norbert's wife and one of his sons deceased, shot in the head.

Three days later, on October 23rd, the Italian police reported having found Norbert and his remaining son shot to death in Norbert's car in the town of Brindisi. It was later ruled a murder-suicide, and Norbert's gun was confirmed to be the murder weapon. His gun was also confirmed to have been the weapon used to kill the other three victims found shot to death in their vehicles.

TWENTY-TWO

Wolfgang Schmidt

THE PINK GIANT

On October 5, 1966, Wolfgang Schmidt was born. Thirty-five years later, Wolfgang changed his name to Beate and began taking hormones and gender reassignment to become a woman. But during those years in between, specifically 1989 to 1991, Wolfgang murdered five women and a three-month-old baby and was dubbed the "Beast of Beelitz" by the media.

On October 24, 1989, Wolfgang Schmidt murdered fifty-one-year-old Edeltraut Nixdorf while she was gardening. Then on May 24, 1990, he raped and strangled forty-five-year-old Christa Naujoks. The following year in 1991, Schmidt raped and beat to death thirty-four-year-old Inge Fischer. A week later, he strangled forty-four-year-old Tamara Petrowskaja to death and killed her three-month-old son. Schmidt's final murder was of sixty-six-year-old Talita Bremer on April 5th that year, where he raped and strangled her to death.

As more details became known about the murders, precisely the fact that the murderer was big in stature and liked to wear pink lingerie, the public nicknamed the murderer the "Pink Giant."

A few months later, in August 1991, two men were out jogging and came across Schmidt masturbating while wearing a bra out in public. Police were called, and Wolfgang was arrested.

In 1992, Schmidt was sentenced to fifteen years in a psychiatric hospital in Brandenberg.

TWENTY-THREE

Martin Ney

THE MASKED MAN

Martin Ney was born on December 12, 1970. He became known by the public and the media as the "Masked Man" in the 1990s and early 2000s.

Boys in the Northern part of Germany were

sexually assaulted at night by a tall, masked man while they were in a school home, youth home, or youth camp. By the time he was caught, there were over forty-five boys sexually assaulted and three murdered.

Assaults

In March 1992, the assaults on boys began in different children's schools located in Hepstedt, Zeven, and Wuisbuttel.

In Hepstedt, a masked man was spotted in an empty dormitory of the children's school but fled. A few days later, the same man tried to sexually assault an eleven-year-old boy at that same school. When the boy began to scream at the top of his lungs, the man fled from the school.

Throughout that Spring and Summer, several of the boys reported that they were woken up by a masked man who was touching them in their beds while they were sleeping. By September, the man was braver. He asked the boys to remove their clothing while he stood over them at their bed. He sexually assaulted three of these boys. The school set up a motion detector and a new door-locking system in the dorms.

At another school home in Zeven, similar

attacks occurred during the same period. Here, the masked man would just pick up the young boy from his bed and carry him into another room, which was empty, and he would assault the boy there. On other occasions, the masked man would wait in the boys' bathrooms until one of them would come into the bathroom stall, and he would touch them. The assaults continued until 1998 at this school.

In the Summers of 1995 and 1999, two boys at another boy's school home in Wuisbuttel were sexually assaulted as well. The masked man entered and exited through the boy's bedroom window.

Also, in 1992, attacks were happening at nearby school camps. Several boys were sexually assaulted by a masked man during the night while in their tents. These attacks went on for almost two years.

Attacks were also happening in family homes. In April 1994, the attacks on three boys in the Bremen area were reported to the police. They all reportedly happened by the same masked man. Even though the parents reported the assault, the police decided it was best not to panic the neighborhood by reporting the crime to the news media.

Murders

In March 1992, thirteen-year-old Stefan Jahr vanished from his bedroom at his boarding school in Scheebel. His body wasn't discovered for five weeks when he was found with his hands tied behind his back and partially buried in a field.

From that same boarding school in April 1992, another boy, eleven-year-old Jonathan Coulom, also went missing. His body was found in a different country, France, a month later. He had been handcuffed to a cement block and thrown into a pond.

In July 1994, eight-year-old Dennis Rostel disappeared from his school camp. His body was found two weeks later by two German tourists in Denmark.

Nine-year-old Dennis Klein went missing from the boy's school in Wuisbuttel sometime during the night on September 5, 2001. He was last seen going to bed the night before. A search began for the boy, who was not found for two weeks when a mushroom picker found his remains while working in his field.

Investigation

After the murder of Dennis Klein, a commission was started to investigate. The police knew some information about the attacker: they described the suspect as a strikingly tall, stocky man with an intense voice who spoke in German. Police also figured he knew the northern regions of Germany quite well because of his actions around the schools and camps. The perpetrator's actions also led police to believe that he was more of a loner and related to young boys easily. He was probably socially integrated with boys in his younger days, feeling comfortable and knowing how to act around them.

Law enforcement conducted several media interviews and released some information regarding the case. They received over eight thousand clues they had to go through and could not find anything.

It wasn't until April 15, 2011, that the police finally arrested Ney after receiving an eyewitness tip and a drawing of a man in a car leaving one of the murder scenes. Ney was not even on the police radar even though he was previously convicted of threatening to kidnap and kill a couple's children in 1989. In that case, he was convicted of the threat, but the record had been taken off the school registry of child threats when Key turned twenty-four years old. In 2005, Ney had also been charged with sexually assaulting two minors. That case was never tried, and the charges were dropped when he agreed to pay the parents 1800 euros. Fortunately, a boy whom Ney had assaulted was able to identify Ney as his assaulter.

After they brought Ney in for questioning, the police searched his apartment and seized his computer. Upon analysis, police found over thirty thousand pictures of children naked and or in sexual situations. Many photos could not be used in court as they were taken years prior and exceeded the statute of limitations.

After only one interrogation, Ney began to confess his crimes. When asked by police why he murdered only three of his over forty victims, Ney said it was because those three boys could identify him, so he had to murder them to avoid being caught. He claimed that he strangled Jahr because he had raped the boy in his car and figured there was a possibility Jahr saw his license plate number. In the case of Klein, Ney smothered him to death with a pillow because he was screaming and resisting, and it seemed to be the only way to get him to stop fighting back.

Key never really explained why he murdered the third boy, Rostel. The only thing he told detectives about the assault was that it was an enjoyable experience. He said they spent three or four days at a guest house in Denmark, and it felt like a vacation.

Trial & Sentencing

On February 27, 2012, Ney's trial finished, and he was sentenced to life imprisonment for the murder of three boys and twenty sexual abuse cases against minors. Initially, the court also added to Ney's sentence a preventative detention stipulation, in which he would never be allowed to receive parole or get out of prison in the future for good behavior. Ney's attorneys filed an appeal a year later and won. The Supreme Court removed the preventative detention stipulation.

TWENTY-FOUR

Marianne Nölle

ANGEL OF MERCY

Marianne Nölle was born in Cologne, Germany, in 1938. As an adult, she became a nurse at her local hospital. After so many of her patients died, she came under suspicion.

In 1993, she was tried and convicted of killing seven of the patients who were in her care between the years 1984 and 1992. She killed them by giving them too much of the drug Truxal, a sedative.

The police believed that she killed seventeen of her patients and attempted to kill more. However, before or during the trial, Nölle refused to answer any questions or admit to doing anything wrong. The prosecutor was only able to prove that Nölle killed seven of the seventeen conclusively.

Regardless, in 1993, Nölle was still sentenced to life imprisonment. She died in 2022 at the age of 84.

TWENTY-FIVE

Frank Gust

THE RHINE-RUHR RIPPER

To the outside world, Frank Gust lived a normal everyday life. He was married with a child. But behind the scenes, he was a serial killer and sexual sadist who eventually became known as the "Rhine-Ruhr-Ripper." The media and the public called him this because of where he killed and the way he murdered his victims was very similar to that of "Jack the Ripper."

Frank Gust was born on May 24, 1969, in Germany. At a very early age, Gust was showing sadistic behavior toward animals. He used to capture small animals such as cats, dogs, and rabbits, tie them up, and torture them before killing them and then dissecting them.

By the age of thirteen, his lust for the dead spread to humans. Gust was breaking into morgues and having sex with the dead women being housed there. When he was caught, Gust confessed to the police that it was his greatest desire to touch the heart of a dying woman. He claimed that he was trying to find a woman who was not yet dead but dying so he could feel their heart as it stopped.

By the age of twenty-six, Gust murdered four women in the West German region known as Rhine-Ruhr. Two of the women were prostitutes, both of whom he picked up at the Essen Central station; one was a South African hitchhiker, and the fourth was the forty-seven aunt of his wife.

The hitchhiker's body was the first victim to be found without her head in a park in Ede. The two prostitutes' bodies were discovered completely mutilated near the train station where he had picked them up. But Gust's aunt's body was never found.

Gust used to leave his victims' bodies in a location where they would be easily found. He wanted people to see the badly tortured bodies.

It wasn't until a friend of Gust's mother went to the police to report him for telling his mother that he had murdered someone that the police started to do an investigation on him. Shortly after that, he was arrested and tried. On September 21, 2000, Gust was convicted of murdering four women and sentenced to life in prison. The court offered Gust complete mental treatment services as well, which Gust took part in for about six months before quitting, saying that there was no point in taking treatment as he would be in prison for life.

TWENTY-SIX

Stephan Letter

ANGEL OF DEATH

Stephan Letter was born on September 17, 1978. He is a serial killer responsible for one of the most significant amount of killings in Germany since World War II. He was convicted of murdering twenty-nine patients while working at a hospital in the city of Sonthofen, Bavaria. Letter started working as a nurse at the hospital in January 2003, caring for older people who needed long-term care. He only worked there for a year and a half before being fired in July 2004.

A high death rate in elderly patients is not usual. So, at first, even though the death rate was higher than usual, there was no real suspicion of the rate or of Letter himself. He first became a person of interest when police were investigating a large number of drugs that had gone missing from the hospital. When they searched Letter's apartment, they found several unused vials of medication, all taken from the hospital.

During the time he was employed there, and more specifically, during his work shifts, there were more than eighty patient deaths. Now, officials were suspicious.

After his arrest for stealing the drugs, law enforcement exhumed the bodies of forty of the patients who had died during his time at the hospital. Unfortunately, the others had been cremated.

Letter was arrested and charged with being responsible for the deaths of twenty-nine people, where the majority of them were over the age of seventy-five and were as old as ninety-four. The charges ended up being sixteen counts of murder, twelve counts of manslaughter, and one count of murder on demand, which meant that someone asked him to kill them.

He was brought to trial in February 2006, and during the trial, Letter said he had committed some of the murders but claimed that some of the patients had asked him to help put them out of their suffering by ending their lives.

The prosecution responded by informing the jury that most of the patients that Letter killed were not only in good health, but several of them were about to be released from the hospital and return home.

The trial lasted ten months, and Letter was found responsible for all twenty-nine of the deaths that he was charged with. He was sentenced to life imprisonment and is now serving out his time in the Strubing prison.

Sources

1. Martingale, Moira: *Cannibal Killers: The Impossible Monsters*. 1993. London. Robert Hale. pp. 34–35. ISBN 0-7090-5034-8
2. "Prostitute Killer Found Dead in His Cell in Germany," July 2, 2007
3. Zeiller (1661) p.303. In an earlier 1640 work, Martin Zeiller notes the existence of a small pamphlet concerning an unnamed murderer at an unidentified place who killed 964 persons, erroneously dating this to 1580, Zeiller (1640), p.232
4. Gesche Gottfried in the German National Library catalog
5. *The Washington Times*. September 19, 1921. FINAL HOME EDITION. Page 3. Image 3
6. "Ein nützlicher Mörder" (in German). Der Spiegel.
7. *Reading Eagle.* Google News Archive Search
8. *Real Life Crimes.* p. 2650, ISBN 1-85875-440-2
9. Richard Plant: *The Pink Triangle.* p. 45. 1986. New York, Henry Holt & Co.
10. *Monsters of Weimar*, p. 99.
11. *Monsters of Weimar*, p. 65.
12. Monsters of Weimar, p. 86.
13. Monsters of Weimar, p. 60.
14. *Monsters of Weimar*, p. 81.
15. *Monsters of Weimar*, p. 54.
16. Möckl, Sybille: ARD-Drama *Mord in Eberswalde*: "Der verheimlichte Serienmörder der DDR." RP ONLINE

17. "Fritz Honka: Der Frauenmörder von St Pauli." NDR.de, Norddeutscher Rundfunk.
18. Wunder, Olaf: "Hamburg historisch Der Tag, an dem Fritz Honka gefasst wurde." 15 April 2012. *Hamburger Morgenpost*
19. Thomas Meiser: http://www.thomas-meiser.de/tcrime/kroll.htm
20. "Nurse Guilty of Killing 28 Patients." *China Daily*.
21. "Angel of Death Nurse Trial Begins." *The Independent*. 8 February 2006.
22. Scott Andrew Selby: *A Serial Killer in Nazi Berlin: The Chilling True Story of the S-Bahn Murderer*. Berkley Publishing Group. 2014. ISBN 978-0-425-26414-0
23. Chalk, Titus; Henze, Jacob; & Malmgren, Sigrid: "The Haunted Sanatorium of Beelitz." May 5, 2011. *Exberliner*.
24. Anna Marie Zwanziger at Serial Killer True Crime Library
25. Kirchschlager, Michael: *Historische Serienmörder*. 2007. ISBN 3-934277-13-6
26. Griffiths, Arthur: *The History and Romance of Crime From the Earliest to the Present Day*. The Grolier Society. 1900. London. pp. 82–90
27. "The Bogeyman's Gonna Eat You–Albert Fish, The Vampire of Brooklyn." *America's Serial Killers: Portraits in Evil*. Mill Creek Entertainment, 2009
28. Fahndungserfolg: Verdächtiger im Fall Dennis gesteht Morde an drei Kindern - DER SPIEGEL
29. Lebenslange Haft für Kindermörder Martin N. (faz.net)
30. Jan Dräger: "Hunt for a serial killer – Almost ten years ago, 9-year-old Dennis was killed. Now

there is a new track." *Die Welt.* 11 February 2011. p. 32
31. "Maskenmann" Martin N.: Kindermörder verrät nach Jahren Passwörter - DER SPIEGEL
32. Friedrichsen, Gisela: "Ein Ausholen zum Gegenschlag" (A knock-out to the counter-strike). November 1992. *Der Spiegel*
33. Becker, Claudia: "Der Serienkiller darf sich ein bisschen frei bewegen" (The serial killer may move a bit freely). *Die Welt.* 16 July 2013
34. Fuchs, Christian: *Bad Blood: An Illustrated Guide to Psycho Cinema.* Creation Books. 1996. ISBN 1-84068-025-3
35. Fred Breinersdorfer, Elke R. Evert: *The Hammer Killer: A Documentary Novel.* 1986. Factor Publishing House. Stuttgart. ISBN 3-925860-00-2
36. "Prostitute Killer Found Dead in His Cell in Germany." *Typically Spanish.* 2 July 2007
37. Tremlett, Giles: "Police Arrest Truck Driver After Six-year Murder Hunt." *Guardian.* November 23, 2006
38. Brückweh, Kerstin: *Mordlust. Serienmorde, Gewalt und Emotionen im 20. Jahrhundert.* ISBN 978-3-593-38202-9
39. Wunder, Olaf: "Hamburg historisch Der Tag, an dem Fritz Honka gefasst wurde" 15 April 2012
40. Ramsland, Katherine: *The Human Predator: A Historical Chronicle of Serial Murder and Forensic Investigation.* 2013. Penguin Books. pp. 284–285. ISBN 978-1101619056
41. Nash, Jay Robert: *World Encyclopedia of 20th Century Murder.* 1992. Rowman & Littlefield. pp. 293–294. ISBN 1590775325

42. "The Case of the Granny Murderer," *Der Spiegel*. 15 December 2008
43. Peter-Philip Schmitt:. "Women Murderer Heinrich Pommerenke, 'The Beast in Human Form,' is Dead." 30 December 2008
44. Busse, Michael: *Before You Sits the Devil*, TV documentary, 2004
45. Zander, Ulrich: "The Beasts of No Man's Land." *Braunschweiger Zeitung*. 30 July 2013
46. Selby, Scott Andrew: *A Serial Killer in Nazi Berlin: The Chilling True Story of the S-Bahn Murderer*. 2014. Berkley Publishing Group.
47. Robinson, Matt: *The S-Bahn Murderer*. 10 April 2021
48. "Butcher Held For Killing Twenty Girls And Selling Flesh." *The Washington Times*. 19 September 1921
49. "German Bluebeard Takes Own Life." *East Mississippi Times*. 14 July 1922
50. "Centipede: Nice enough to eat; Cannibals of the 20th century." *The Guardian*. 20 May 1993. p. 12.
51. Berg, Karl: *The Sadist*. 1938. ISBN 978-9-333-35227-7
52. Berg, Karl; Godwin, George: *Monsters of Weimar: Kürten, the Vampire of Düsseldorf*. 1937. ISBN 1-897743-10-6
53. Cawthorne, Nigel; Tibballs, Geoffrey: *Killers: The Ruthless Exponents of Murder*. 1993. ISBN 0-7522-0850-0
54. Elder, Sace: *Murder Scenes: Normality, Deviance, and Criminal Violence in Weimar Berlin*. 2010. ISBN 978-0-472-11724-6
55. Lane, Brian; Gregg, Wilfred: *The Encyclopedia of Serial Killers*. 1992. ISBN 978-0-747-23731-0

56. Nash, Jay Robert: *The Great Pictorial History of World Crime*, Volume 2. 2004. ISBN 978-1-461-71215-2

About the Author

Alan R Warren is a Bestselling Author, Producer, and host of the popular NBC Radioshow *House of Mystery* and *Inside Writing*, both heard on the 106.5 F.M. Los Angeles/102.3 F.M. Riverside/ 1050 A.M. Palm Springs/ 540 A.M. KYAH Salt Lake City/ 1150 A.M. KKNW Seattle/Tacoma and Phoenix.

His bestselling true crime books in Canada include *Beyond Suspicion: The True Story of Colonel Russell Williams*, which will be featured on CNN's *Lies, Crimes, & Videos* (Season 4), and *Murder Times Six: The True Story of the Wells Gray Park Murders*. In America, his bestsellers include *The Killing Game: Serial Killer Rodney Alcala*, which was featured on several television shows such as *Very Scary People with Donny Walberg*, Oxygen's *Mark of a Killer*, Reelz' *Killer Trophies*, and soon to be included in a four-part Sundance Channel documentary called *Death's Date*. His bestseller, *Doomsday Cults: The Devil's Hostages*, was featured on Vice's *Dark Side of the '90s*.

His latest series, *Killer Queens*, is a six-part book series covering murders that affect the Gay Community. So far, it includes Book 1 - Leopold & Loeb, Book 2 - Butcher of Hanover: Fritz Haarmann, Book 3 - Grindr Serial Killer: Stephen Port, and Book 4 - Bruce McArthur: Toronto Gay Killer.

Also By Alan R. Warren

Beyond Suspicion: Russell Williams – A Canadian Serial Killer

Young girl's panties started to go missing; sexual assaults began to occur, and then female bodies were found! Soon this quiet town of Tweed, Ontario, was in a panic. What is even more shocking was when an upstanding resident stood accused of the assaults. This was not just any man, but a pillar of the community; a decorated military pilot who had flown Canadian Forces VIP aircraft for dignitaries such as the Queen of England, Prince Philip, the Governor-General and Prime Minister of Canada.

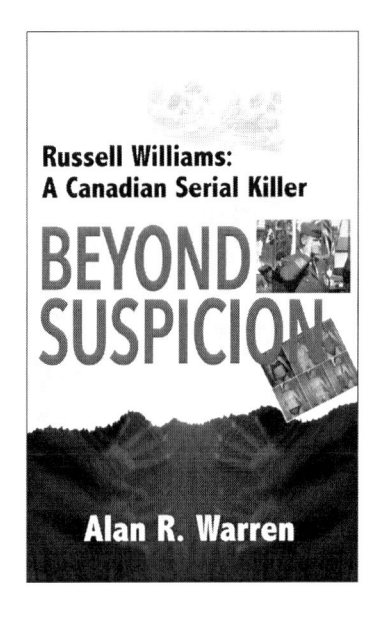

This is the story of serial killer Russell Williams, the elite pilot of Canada's Air Force One, and the innocent victims he murdered. Unlike other serial killers, Williams seemed very unaffected about his crimes and leading two different lives.

Alan R. Warren describes the secret life including the

abductions, rape, and murders that were unleashed on an unsuspecting community. Included are letters written to the victims by Williams and descriptions of the assaults and rapes as seen on videos and photos taken by Williams during the attacks.

This updated version also contains the full brilliant police interrogation of Williams and his confession. Also, the twisted way the Williams planned to pin his crimes on his unsuspecting neighbor.

Doomsday Cults: The Devil's Hostages

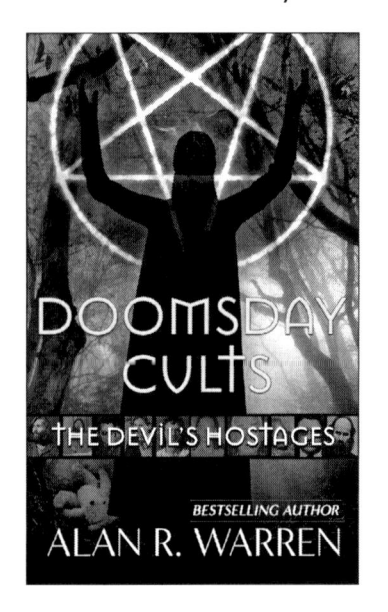

Jim Jones convinced his 1000 followers they would all have to commit suicide since he was going to die. Shoko Asahara convinced his followers to release a weapon of mass destruction, the deadly sarin gas, on a Tokyo subway. The Order of the Solar Temple lured the rich and famous, including Princess Grace of Monaco, and convinced them to die a fiery death now on Earth to be reborn on a better planet called Sirius. Charles Manson convinced his followers to kill, in an attempt to incite an apocalyptic race war.

These are a few of the doomsday cults examined in this

book by bestselling author Alan R. Warren. Its focus is on cults whose destructive behavior was due in large part to their apocalyptic beliefs or doomsday movements. It includes details surrounding the massacres and a look into how their members became so brainwashed they committed unimaginable crimes at the command of their leader.

Usually, when we hear about these cults and their massacres, we ask ourselves how it possibly happened. We could also ask ourselves, what then is the difference between a cult and a religion? We once had a small group of people who unquestionably followed a person who believed he was the son of God. Two thousand years later, that following is one of the most recognized religions in the world. This book in no way criticizes believing in God. Rather, it examines how a social movement grows into a full religion and when it does not. And what makes the conventional faiths such as Christianity, Judaism, Islam, and Hinduism stand above groups such as the Branch Davidians or Children of God.

In Chains: The Dangerous World of Human Trafficking

Human trafficking is the trade of people for forced labor or sex. It also includes the illegal extraction of human organs and tissues. And it is an extremely ruthless and dangerous industry plaguing our world today.

Most believe human trafficking occurs in countries with no human rights legislation. This is a myth. All types of human trafficking are alive and well in most of the developed countries of the world like the United States, Canada, and the UK. It is estimated that $150 billion a year is generated in the forced labor industry alone. It is also believed that 21 million people are trapped in modern-day slavery – exploited for sex, labor, or organs.

Most also believe since they live in a free country, there is built-in protection against such illegal practices. But for many, this is not the case. Traffickers tend to focus on the most vulnerable in our society, but trafficking can happen to anyone. You will see how easy it can happen in the stories included in "In Chains."

BUTCHER OF HANOVER: Fritz Haarmann (Killer Queens 2)

Killer Queens is a new series of historical fiction books based on true stories. Sources, such as police reports and newspaper articles, are examined to gather as many facts as possible surrounding each case. As with any work of fiction, some creative additions are made when telling these stories, usually within the conversations between the personalities involved. The various sources are the basis of these conversations and hopefully, make them come alive for the readers to help understand what was meant by those words.

Book 2 of the series focuses on the serial killer of at least twenty-seven young men and boys in Germany in the post-World War 1 era. At the center of this murder case were Fritz Haarmann and Hans Grans, who were lovers while committing these murders. It wasn't until the skulls and bones started washing ashore from the Leine River in Hanover that Germany realized they had a cold-blooded serial killer in their country.

Unlike Leopold and Loeb murder case covered in Book 1, where the dominance shifted from one to the other, Fritz Haarmann was the dominant partner in this case. He carried out each of the murders and dismemberment of the bodies himself, even though he claimed that Grans chose who was to be murdered in court.

As you read the exploration of the case in this book, ask yourself, did Haarmann murder each victim to keep his lover Hans Grans to stay with him? Did Grans decide who it was that was to be murdered? The evidence on this case will keep you on the edge of your seat, trying to determine who was really behind these gruesome murders.

MURDER TIMES SIX: The True Story of The Wells Park Murders

"The author even had me (who conducted the interview) on the edge of my seat as I was turning the pages as "the Detective" was trying to unearth the unspeakable truth."

Sgt. Mike Eastham R.C.M.P.

It was a crime unlike anything seen in British Columbia. The horror of the "Wells Gray Murders" almost forty years ago transcends decades.

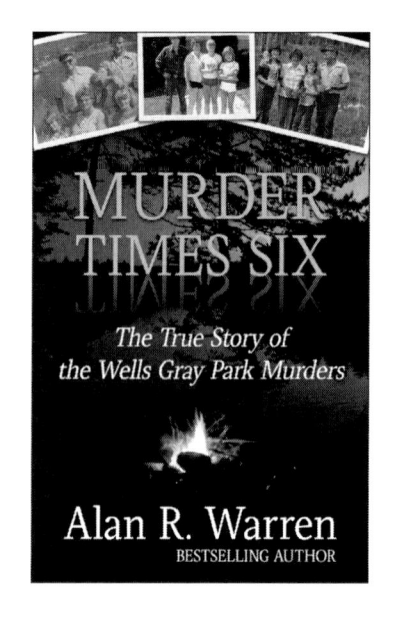

On August 2, 1982, three generations of a family set out on a camping trip – Bob and Jackie Johnson, their two daughters, Janet, 13 and Karen, 11, and Jackie's parents, George and Edith Bentley. A month later, the Johnson family car was found off a mountainside logging road near Wells Gray Park completely burned out. In the back seat were the incinerated remains of four adults, and in the trunk were the two girls.

But this was not just your average mass murder. It was much worse. Over time, some brutal details were revealed; however, most are still only known to the murderer, David Ennis (formerly Shearing). His crimes had far-reaching impacts on the family, community, and country. It still does today. Every time Shearing attempts freedom from the parole board, the grief is triggered as everyone is forced to relive the horrors once again.

Murder Times Six shines a spotlight on the crime that captured the attention of a nation, recounts the narrative of a complex police investigation, and discusses whether a convicted mass murderer should ever be allowed to leave the confines of an institution. Most importantly, it tells the story of one family forever changed.

Manufactured by Amazon.ca
Acheson, AB